Sabrina Barker

KETO Air Fryer Cookbook

Easy Low Carb Snacks & Meals for Beginners and Advanced Users. Quick, Tasty and Ketogenic Diet Recipes for Carefree Weight Loss and Healthy Lifestyle

Disclaimer Notice:

This cookbook is provided for informational purposes only and does not constitute legal, medical, or professional advice of any kind. The recipes and tips contained herein are provided "as is" and the author and publisher disclaim all warranties, express or implied, including any warranty of accuracy, completeness, or fitness for a particular purpose. The use of the information provided in this book is solely at the reader's risk. The author and publisher shall not be liable for any damages, including but not limited to special, incidental, consequential, or other damages. Readers are encouraged to consult with a professional when necessary and to use their discretion while following the recipes and advice contained in this book.

Table of Contents

Chapter 1:

Introduction

Welcome to a culinary adventure that promises not just to change the way you eat but to transform your approach to healthy living! I'm Sabrina Barker, your guide on this delicious journey. As a fitness trainer, nutritionist, and mom of three, I've discovered the power of the keto diet and air frying to create meals that are not only nutritious and low-carb but also incredibly tasty and satisfying.

This cookbook is more than just a collection of recipes it's a gateway to a lifestyle that embraces healthy fats, nutrient-rich foods, and the simplicity and convenience of your air fryer. Whether you're new to the keto diet, looking to shed a few pounds, or simply searching for meal inspiration that aligns with a low-carb lifestyle, you've come to the right place.

Inside, you'll find a wide range of recipes—from quick and easy snacks to sophisticated main dishes and delectable desserts—that cater to beginners and advanced keto enthusiasts alike. Each recipe is designed to be easy to follow, with ingredients you can find in your local supermarket, ensuring you can enjoy the benefits of keto cooking without any hassle.

But this book is about much more than just food. It's a treasure trove of bonuses, secrets, and tips—a compilation of culinary discoveries and keto hacks that will enrich your cooking experience. From uncovering the secrets to making the perfect keto bread to demystifying the art of low-carb desserts, this book is packed with insights that will make healthy eating enjoyable and accessible.

It's about finding joy in the kitchen and the satisfaction that comes from feeding yourself and your loved ones meals that are good for the body and the soul. So, are you ready to embark on a culinary journey that will tantalize your taste buds, nourish your body, and unveil a world of healthy cooking secrets? Let's turn the page and start this flavorful adventure together!

Chapter 2:

What is the Keto Diet?

2.1 Keto Evolution: Historical Insights and Scientific Evidence

Ever wonder how the keto diet, which now stars in our kitchens and social feeds, came to be? It's a journey that's as fascinating as the diet itself. Let's dive into a quick history lesson and some science behind why keto works wonders for so many.

- **A Trip Down Memory Lane:** The keto diet isn't a modern fad; it's been around since the 1920s, initially used as a treatment for epilepsy. Doctors noticed that fasting helped control seizures, leading to the development of a diet that mimicked the effects of fasting. Fast forward, and keto has evolved into a powerhouse for weight loss and health improvement.
- **Science Speaks Volumes:** At its core, keto is about changing how your body fuels itself, switching from carbs to fats. This switch flips your metabolic switch, leading to ketosis, where your body becomes incredibly efficient at burning fat for energy. The result? Weight loss, improved energy, and a host of other benefits backed by science.
- **Why It Works:** Beyond weight loss, keto has shown promise in improving blood sugar levels, enhancing brain function, and even reducing symptoms of certain chronic diseases. It's the subject of ongoing research, but the evidence so far points to keto being more than just another diet trend.
- **Tailored for Today:** While the basics of keto remain the same, today's keto diet has been adapted to fit our modern lifestyle. It's more flexible, allowing for a wider variety of foods and fitting into our busy lives, proving that good health doesn't have to be complicated.

Intrigued? I sure was when I started my keto journey. It's not just about eating differently; it's about rethinking our relationship with food and fueling our bodies in a way that supports our health and happiness.

Let's keep exploring together how keto can fit into your life and maybe even transform it. Onward to the next chapter!

2.2 Types of Ketogenic Diet

Diving into the keto world, you'll find it's not a one-size-fits-all. There are several variations of the ketogenic diet, each tailored to different lifestyles and goals. Let's explore the types to find your perfect keto fit!

- **Standard Ketogenic Diet (SKD):** The classic keto diet most are familiar with – high in fat (70-75%), moderate in protein (20-25%), and very low in carbs (5-10%). It's the go-to for beginners and those focused on steady weight loss.
- **Cyclical Ketogenic Diet (CKD):** Ideal for athletes and bodybuilders, CKD involves periods of higher-carb refeeds, such as 5 ketogenic days followed by 2 high-carb days. It supports intense workouts and muscle recovery.
- **Targeted Ketogenic Diet (TKD):** This version allows you to add carbs around workouts, offering the energy needed for high-intensity activities. Perfect for those who need a bit more fuel but want to stay in ketosis.
- **High-Protein Ketogenic Diet:** Similar to SKD, but with more protein (60% fat, 35% protein, and 5% carbs). It's favored by those looking to maintain muscle mass while losing fat.
- **Lazy Keto:** Focusing only on keeping carbohydrate intake under a certain threshold (typically under 20 grams a day) without tracking other macronutrients closely. This approach is favored for its simplicity.
- **Dirty Keto:** Similar to the standard ketogenic diet in macronutrient distribution, but not as strict about the quality of foods consumed. Processed foods and artificial sweeteners may be included, making it a controversial choice for health-conscious individuals.

Each type of keto diet has its unique benefits and can be customized to fit your lifestyle and goals. Remember, the key to a successful keto journey is finding the right balance that works for you, and sometimes, a little experimentation is part of the fun. Ready to find your keto type? Let's make this journey delicious and effective together!

2.3 Who Needs the Keto Diet?

Ever wondered if keto is the right fit for you? Well, the beauty of keto is its versatility and ability to cater to a wide range of health and wellness goals. Whether you're a busy bee, a fitness enthusiast, or someone dealing with specific health conditions, keto might just be the lifestyle change you've been looking for. Let's break it down:

- **For the Weight Watchers:** If you're aiming to shed some pounds and have struggled with traditional diets, keto offers a fat-burning solution that could rev up your weight loss journey.
- **Fitness Lovers and Athletes:** Looking to enhance your performance and endurance? Keto could provide the sustained energy you need to smash those fitness goals.
- **Health-Conscious Individuals:** From improving blood sugar levels to increasing good cholesterol

(HDL), keto has shown potential benefits for heart health and diabetes management.

- **Brain Health Advocates:** Experiencing brain fog? The keto diet is known for its ability to enhance mental clarity and cognitive function, making it a favorite among those seeking a mental boost.
- **People with Specific Dietary Needs:** Whether it's gluten intolerance or a sugar-free lifestyle you're after, keto's emphasis on fats and proteins over carbs makes it adaptable for various dietary restrictions.

Remember, while keto offers numerous benefits, it's important to consult with a healthcare professional before making any significant changes to your diet, especially if you have existing health conditions. Ready to see if keto can make a difference in your life? Let's dive deeper and discover how to tailor it to fit your unique needs.

2.4 Benefits of the Keto Diet

Ready to discover the transformative power of keto? This lifestyle isn't just about losing weight—it's about gaining a wealth of health benefits that can change your life. Let's dive into the incredible benefits that have made me and countless others keto devotees:

- **Effortless Weight Loss:** Keto isn't just a diet; it's a fat-burning strategy. By turning fat into your primary fuel source, you'll see the pounds melt away without feeling starved.
- **Stabilized Energy Levels:** Forget the mid-afternoon crashes. Keto provides a steady stream of energy from morning to night, thanks to its reliance on fats for fuel.
- **Enhanced Mental Clarity:** Ever feel like you're walking through the fog? Keto clears that right up, boosting your brain function and keeping you sharp and focused.
- **Reduced Inflammation:** Many of us live with chronic inflammation without even knowing it. Keto has been shown to reduce inflammation markers, offering relief from various conditions.
- **Improved Heart Health:** Lowering your intake of carbs can lead to a significant reduction in blood pressure and bad cholesterol levels, paving the way for a healthier heart.
- **Controlled Blood Sugar and Insulin Levels:** For those managing diabetes or at risk of developing it, keto can be a game-changer in regulating blood sugar and insulin levels.
- **Increased Longevity and Overall Health:** Emerging research suggests that keto can not only extend your lifespan but also improve the quality of your life by preventing chronic diseases.

Embarking on a keto journey can seem daunting at first, but the rewards are well worth the effort. From shedding pounds to gaining energy and improving your overall health, the benefits of keto are profound and far-reaching. I've witnessed these changes in myself and in many others. Ready to give it a try and see how your life transforms? Let's keep moving forward together!

2.5 Guidelines for the Keto Diet

Embarking on the keto journey can feel like setting sail into uncharted waters, but fear not! I'm here to guide you through some tried-and-true guidelines that will help make your transition to keto as smooth as possible. Here's how to steer your keto ship with confidence:

- **Start with Your 'Why':** Before diving into keto, clarify your goals. Are you looking to lose weight, improve your energy, or manage your health condition? Your 'why' will be your anchor, keeping you motivated.
- **Simplify Your Kitchen:** Clear out the carb clutter. Stock your pantry with keto essentials like high-quality fats, low-carb veggies, and plenty of protein. A clean and organized kitchen is your first step toward success.
- **Master Your Macros:** Get familiar with the keto macro ratios—roughly 70% fats, 25% protein, and 5% carbs. Apps or online calculators can be a big help in keeping you on track.
- **Hydration is Key:** Keto can initially lead to water loss, so keeping hydrated is crucial. Don't forget to replenish electrolytes like sodium, potassium, and magnesium, too.
- **Plan, Plan, Plan:** Meal planning isn't just a lifesaver; it's a keto success strategy. Knowing what you're going to eat in advance prevents carb temptations and last-minute unhealthy choices.
- **Embrace Experimentation:** Not all keto foods will be love at first bite, and that's okay! Experiment with different recipes and foods to find what you enjoy and what makes you feel best.
- **Connect with Community:** Whether it's joining online forums, following keto influencers for inspiration, or finding a keto buddy, community support can make all the difference.
- **Be Kind to Yourself:** Remember, it's a journey. There will be ups and downs, but every step forward is progress. Celebrate your victories, learn from any setbacks, and keep moving forward.

With these guidelines, you're well on your way to keto success. Remember, it's about making sustainable changes that fit your lifestyle and help you achieve your health goals. Ready to take the next step in your keto journey? Let's do it together!

2.6 Keto Diet Food Guide: What to Eat, What to Limit, and Pantry Staples

Transitioning to a keto lifestyle can seem like navigating a new culinary world. But don't worry, I've got your back! Let's simplify what to stock in your kitchen and what to pass up. Embracing keto is all about making informed choices, so here's your go-to guide:

What to Embrace:

- **Healthy Fats and Oils:** Think avocados, coconut oil, grass-fed butter, and olive oil. These will become your new best friends, providing energy and keeping you satisfied.

- **Proteins:** Choose grass-fed meats, wild-caught fish, and free-range poultry. Remember, keto is a high-fat moderate protein, so keep an eye on those protein portions.
- **Low-Carb Vegetables:** Fill your plate with leafy greens, broccoli, zucchini, and bell peppers. They're packed with nutrients and won't kick you out of ketosis.
- **Nuts and Seeds:** Almonds, macadamias, flaxseeds, and chia seeds are great for snacks or as additions to meals for extra crunch and nutrients.
- **Dairy:** Full-fat cheeses, heavy cream, and butter are on the menu. They add flavor and richness to your dishes.

What to Limit:

- **Sugary Foods and Drinks:** This includes soda, candy, and baked goods made with refined sugars. They're a big no-no on keto.
- **Grains:** Bread, pasta, rice, and cereals are high in carbs and not keto-friendly.
- **Starchy Vegetables:** Potatoes, corn, and peas are high in carbs and best avoided.
- **Most Fruits:** Except for small portions of berries, most fruits are too high in sugar for the keto diet.

Pantry Staples:

- **Spices and Herbs:** They add flavor without the carbs. Get creative with seasonings to keep your meals interesting.
- **Low-Carb Sweeteners:** Stevia, erythritol, and monk fruit can satisfy your sweet tooth without the carb count.
- **Low-Carb Flours:** Almond and coconut flour can replace traditional flour for your baking needs.

Remember, the key to a successful keto diet is preparation and knowing your foods. With this guide, you'll be well on your way to enjoying delicious, keto-friendly meals that support your health goals. Happy keto cooking!

2.7 How to Prepare Your Keto Lifestyle

Embarking on a keto lifestyle is an exciting journey of transformation and discovery. It's not just about changing what you eat; it's about changing how you live. Ready to make keto a part of your life? Here are some steps to get you started on the right foot:

- **Embrace the Learning Curve:** First things first, immerse yourself in all things keto. Read books, follow keto blogs, and join online communities. Knowledge is power, and the more you know, the easier your transition will be.
- **Kitchen Makeover:** Out with the old, in with the new! Clear your kitchen of high-carb temptations and stock up on keto-friendly staples. Think of it as setting the stage for your new lifestyle.
- **Meal Planning Mastery:** One of the keys to keto success is planning. Start by planning your meals for the week. This not only helps you stay on track but also saves time and reduces stress.

- **Get Creative in the Kitchen:** The keto diet is incredibly versatile. Experiment with new recipes and find fun ways to enjoy your favorite foods in a keto-friendly format. Cauliflower pizza, anyone?
- **Track Your Progress:** Keeping a food diary or using a tracking app can help you monitor your macros and stay within your daily limits. It's also a great way to see how far you've come.
- **Find Your Support System:** Whether it's friends, family, or an online community, having support can make all the difference. Share your goals, celebrate your wins, and lean on your support system when you need it.
- **Listen to Your Body:** Everyone's experience with keto is unique. Pay attention to how your body responds and be willing to adjust your approach as needed. Remember, this is a lifestyle, not a race.
- **Enjoy the Journey:** Lastly, have fun with it! Explore new foods, enjoy the process of cooking, and discover what works best for you. Celebrate your successes, no matter how small they may seem.

By following these steps, you're not just adopting a diet; you're embracing a lifestyle that prioritizes health, well-being, and joy. I'm here with you every step of the way, ready to share tips, recipes, and encouragement. Let's do this together!

2.8 10 Easy Swaps to Make Keto

Starting a keto diet doesn't mean you have to give up on your favorite foods. It's all about smart swaps that keep your meals delicious and keto-friendly. Here are my top 10 swaps that make sticking to the keto lifestyle a breeze:

1. **Cauliflower for Rice:** Swap out white rice for cauliflower rice to cut carbs and add a serving of veggies to your meal.
2. **Zoodles instead of Pasta:** Spiralized zucchini makes a fantastic pasta substitute, satisfying your noodle cravings without the carb overload.
3. **Lettuce Wraps over Bread:** Use lettuce leaves as wraps for your next sandwich or burger to keep it light and low-carb.
4. **Nut Flours for Wheat Flour:** Almond and coconut flour are great for baking and cooking, offering a low-carb alternative to traditional flours.
5. **Sugar Alternatives:** Sweeten your dishes with stevia or erythritol instead of sugar to keep your carbs in check.
6. **Avocado instead of Mayo:** Creamy avocado can replace mayonnaise in sandwiches and salads, adding healthy fats and nutrients.
7. **Seeds and Nuts instead of Crunchy Snacks:** For a crunchy snack, opt for seeds and nuts instead of chips or crackers.
8. **Unsweetened Almond Milk over Regular Milk:** Lower in carbs and calories, unsweetened almond milk is a great substitute for regular dairy milk.
9. **Greek Yogurt instead of Sour Cream:** Full-fat Greek yogurt can replace sour cream for a protein-packed, low-carb alternative.
10. **Berries instead of High-Sugar Fruits:** Enjoy berries in moderation for a sweet treat that won't kick you out of ketosis.

Embracing these swaps can make your keto journey enjoyable and sustainable. Remember, it's about finding what works for you and making adjustments that fit your lifestyle. Happy swapping!

2.9 Keto Desserts Explained: Understanding Keto-Friendly Sweets

Today, let's debunk the myth that going keto means saying goodbye to desserts. In the keto world, we just get a little creative and still indulge in delicious sweets that align with our health goals. Here's how you can have your cake (and eat it, too!) on a keto diet:

- **Embrace Natural Sweeteners:** Forget about sugar; natural sweeteners like stevia, erythritol, and monk fruit are your new best friends. They're sweet, keto-friendly, and don't impact your blood sugar levels.
- **Flour Power:** Traditional flour is out, but almond and coconut flour are in! They're low in carbs and perfect for baking your favorite treats.
- **Fat is Fab:** In keto desserts, fats like butter, coconut oil, and cream cheese not only add richness but also help you feel satisfied. Plus, they make everything taste better!
- **Fruitful Choices:** While most fruits are off-limits due to high sugar content, berries are a great exception. Use them to add natural sweetness and a burst of flavor to your desserts.
- **Chocolate Dreams:** Good news for chocolate lovers dark chocolate (with high cocoa content and low sugar) is keto-friendly. It's perfect for those moments when only chocolate will do.
- **Portion Control:** Even with keto desserts, it's all about balance. Enjoy them in moderation to satisfy your sweet tooth without overdoing it.
- **Experiment and Enjoy:** The best part about keto desserts is experimenting with different recipes and finding what you love. From cheesecakes to brownies and everything in between, there's a keto version of almost every dessert.

Remember, living a keto lifestyle doesn't mean you have to sacrifice enjoyment of food, especially desserts. With these tips, you can enjoy sweet treats that are not only delicious but also support your keto journey. So go ahead, whip up something sweet, and enjoy every bite guilt-free!

2.10 Flavorful Keto: Zero-Carb Ways to Elevate Your Meals

How to zest up your keto meals without adding a single carb? Who says keto food has to be bland? Not on my watch! Here are some flavorful, zero-carb ways to make every meal a taste adventure:

- **Spices and Herbs:** These are your culinary secret weapons. From basil and oregano to cumin and curry, they add a world of flavor without the carbs.
- **Citrus Zest:** A little zest from lemons or limes can brighten up any dish, adding freshness and tang without sugar.

- **Infused Oils:** Elevate your cooking with oils infused with garlic, chili, or herbs. They're a fantastic way to add depth to your dishes.
- **Vinegars:** Apple cider, white, and red wine vinegars can add a punch of flavor to salads and cooked dishes, all carb-free.
- **Mustards:** From Dijon to whole grain, mustards are a great way to add complexity and tanginess to your meals.
- **Cocoa Powder:** For a rich, chocolatey flavor without the sweetness, a sprinkle of unsweetened cocoa powder goes a long way in desserts and even some savory dishes.
- **Extracts:** Vanilla, almond, and peppermint extracts can add a burst of flavor to your baking and beverages without any carbs.
- **Cheese:** Strong cheeses like Parmesan, blue cheese, and aged cheddar add a lot of flavors and are perfect for sprinkling over dishes.
- **Nuts and Seeds:** Toast them to bring out their flavor and add them to salads, yogurt, or as a crunchy topping for any dish.
- **Aminos and Sauces:** Coconut aminos, hot sauce, and Worcestershire sauce can add layers of flavor without the added sugar found in traditional sauces.

With these zero-carb flavor boosters, your keto meals will never be dull. Remember, the key to a delicious keto diet is creativity and willingness to experiment. Happy cooking, and let's keep making keto delicious together!

2.11 Keto Curiosities: Fascinating Facts and Myths

There's a lot of information out there, and not all of it is true. Let's dive into some keto curiosities, separating fact from fiction:

Fact: Keto Has Been Around for a Century: Originally developed in the 1920s to treat epilepsy in children, the keto diet has a long medical history before it became popular for weight loss.

Myth: Keto is Just Another High-Protein Diet: Unlike diets that emphasize protein, keto focuses on fat as the primary source of calories, aiming for a high-fat, moderate-protein, and low-carb ratio.

Fact: Keto Can Improve Brain Function: Beyond weight loss, keto has been shown to offer benefits for brain health, potentially improving cognitive function and even aiding in the treatment of neurological diseases.

Myth: Eating Fat Makes You Fat: One of the biggest misconceptions about keto is that the high fat intake will lead to weight gain. However, when following a keto diet correctly, your body burns fat for energy, often resulting in weight loss.

Fact: Keto Can Lead to Rapid Weight Loss Initially: Many people experience quick weight loss when starting keto, mainly due to water loss as the body adapts to a low-carb intake.

Myth: Keto Is Unsustainable in the Long Term: While it's true that keto requires commitment, many find it sustainable and enjoyable with the right planning and mindset.

Fact: Not All Fats Are Created Equal: On keto, emphasis is placed on healthy fats from sources like avocados, nuts, and olive oil rather than trans fats or highly processed fats.

Myth: You Can Eat Unlimited Calories on Keto and Still Lose Weight. Calorie intake still matters on keto. Overeating, even on a low-carb diet, can hinder weight loss efforts.

Understanding these facts and myths can help you navigate your keto journey more effectively. Remember, everyone's body reacts differently, and what works for one person may not work for another. Stay curious, stay informed, and most importantly, enjoy the journey to a healthier you!

2.12 Keto Tips

1. **Start Now:** Begin your keto journey today; small steps lead to significant changes.
2. **More Salt (Electrolytes):** Increase salt intake to balance electrolytes, enhancing energy and preventing keto flu.
3. **Workouts ≠ Cheat Meals:** Exercise to enhance your keto journey, not as an excuse for off-plan eating.
4. **Intermittent Fasting and Keto:** Combines the benefits of both for improved health and fat burning.
5. **Avoid Exogenous Ketones:** Achieve ketosis naturally through diet for sustainable health benefits.
6. **Be Cautious with 'Keto' Labeled Products:** Not all "keto" products meet strict dietary guidelines; always read labels.
7. **Supplements:** Consider magnesium, omega-3s, and vitamin D supplements to fill nutritional gaps and enhance health.
8. **Sleep Importance:** Aim for 7-9 hours of restful sleep to support hormonal balance and metabolic health on keto.
9. **Alcohol on Keto:** Opt for dry wines, light beers, or spirits with zero-calorie mixers, consumed moderately to fit a keto lifestyle.
10. **If You Slip Up, Don't Give Up:** Mistakes are learning opportunities; keep going.

Chapter 3:

What is the air fryer?

3.1 Understanding Air Frying Technology

Let's dive into one of my favorite kitchen revolutions—the air fryer. This magical device has changed the game for healthy cooking, especially for us in the keto community. But what exactly is an air fryer?

At its core, an air fryer is a compact countertop appliance that uses rapid air circulation technology to cook food. It essentially mimics the results of deep-frying but without the need for copious amounts of oil. This means you can achieve that crave-worthy crispiness with just a fraction of the fat—a dream come true for anyone looking to cut down on unhealthy fats without sacrificing flavor.

The beauty of the air fryer lies in its versatility. From crispy chicken wings and succulent pork chops to tender vegetables and even low-carb bread, there's hardly anything it can't handle. It's fast, it's efficient, and it keeps the unnecessary calories at bay.

So, why does the air fryer earn a special place in the hearts of keto enthusiasts? Let's find out.

3.2 Perfect Match: Keto & Air Fryer

The keto diet emphasizes high-fat, moderate-protein, and low-carb intake to push the body into a state of ketosis, where it burns fat for fuel instead of carbohydrates. Here's where the air fryer shines:

- **Perfect for High-Fat Cooking:** The air fryer allows us to embrace healthy fats without overdoing it. You can cook with a minimal amount of oil and still get that satisfying crunch and texture that usually comes from traditional frying methods.
- **Keeps Carbs in Check:** Since the air fryer is ideal for cooking meats and vegetables, it naturally aligns with the keto diet's low-carb requirements. It makes it easy to whip up delicious, nutritious meals without worrying about carb counts.
- **Innovative Keto Recipes:** The air fryer opens up a world of culinary creativity for keto followers. From air-fried avocado fries to keto-friendly donuts, the possibilities are endless, allowing you to explore a variety of dishes that keep your diet interesting and enjoyable.

- **Time and Energy Efficient:** In our busy lives, the air fryer is a lifesaver. It cooks food faster than traditional ovens and stovetops, saving you time and energy—both of which are precious commodities for anyone juggling a hectic schedule.

In short, the air fryer is not just an appliance it's a tool that empowers keto dieters to maintain their lifestyle with ease and pleasure. It encourages healthier cooking methods, supports dietary restrictions, and unleashes culinary creativity, making it an indispensable ally in your keto journey.

So, are you ready to make the most out of your air fryer and explore the delicious possibilities it holds for your keto lifestyle? Let's get cooking and turn those keto dreams into crispy, tasty realities!

3.3 Air Fryer Tips

- **Quick and Even Cooking:** Kickstart your keto creations by preheating your air fryer. This simple step ensures faster cooking and saves precious minutes. While prepping your ingredients, let the air fryer warm up. Just remember, there is no parchment paper during this phase. It sets the stage for evenly cooked, crispy delights every time.
- **Start with Affordable Basics:** Experiment with economical and simple foods. This way, you can practice air frying techniques without the worry of costly mistakes.
- **Opting for High-Smoke Point Oils:** The secret to perfect air frying? Using oils like avocado, coconut, or high-quality olive oil. These gems can handle the heat, making them ideal for getting that golden crisp without breaking down and affecting the flavor or nutrition of your keto-friendly dishes.
- **Spray Bottles Over Aerosols:** Swap out store-bought aerosols for a simple, refillable oil spray bottle. It's an eco-friendly way to coat your food lightly and evenly without added chemicals. Plus, it ensures your air fryer basket remains in top-notch condition, keeping those keto meals as healthy as they are delicious.
- **Use Heat-Safe Surfaces for Hot Baskets:** Protect your countertops by placing a wooden board or silicone mat under the hot air fryer basket when removed. These surfaces safeguard against heat damage and provide a stable area for handling hot food safely.
- **Avoid Overcrowding:** Think of your air fryer as a mini convection oven—air circulation is its superpower. Packing food too tightly? You'll steam instead of crisp. For that perfect keto crunch, give your goodies room to breathe and cook in batches if needed. This way, every bite is as satisfying as intended.
- **Master the Mid-Cook Toss:** Halfway through cooking, give those keto treats in your air fryer a quick shake or flip. This simple maneuver ensures every piece cooks evenly, getting you that uniform crispiness we all crave. It's a small step with a big impact on texture and taste.
- **Regularly Check Your Food:** Don't just sit and forget. Open the air fryer and check your food periodically to ensure it's cooking evenly and not overcooking.
- **Adjust Times and Temps as Needed:** View air fryer recipe times and temperatures as starting points, not absolutes. Your air fryer's unique characteristics might require slight adjustments. Experimentation is key to finding the perfect settings for your specific model and the dishes you love.
- **Optimize with Parchment Paper:** Enhance your air frying with parchment paper specifically designed for air fryers, complete with holes to maintain airflow. It's a game-changer for easy cleanup and prevent-

ing stickiness. Secure it with heat-resistant magnets or simply place food on top to keep it in place. This smart hack keeps your air fryer clean and your meals perfectly cooked.

- **Foil for Cleanliness and Convenience:** Placing aluminum foil under the air fryer basket can be a clever move for easier cleanup. It catches drips and crumbs, keeping your air fryer base spotless. However, ensure proper airflow by not covering the entire bottom or vents, as this could affect cooking performance.
- **Post-Cooking Clean-Up is Key:** Keep your air fryer in prime condition by cleaning it after every use. This routine prevents buildup and keeps flavors fresh. For those rare but necessary times, gently wiping the heating element can help maintain optimal performance, ensuring even cooking and extending the lifespan of your device.
- **Absorbing Grease and Smoke:** Placing a few pieces of bread and a little water at the bottom of your air fryer's pan can work wonders for catching excess grease and reducing smoke during cooking. This neat trick helps keep your kitchen air cleaner and your air fryer easier to clean, especially when cooking fatty foods.
- **Revitalize Leftovers:** Turn your air fryer into a reheating magician. It's perfect for bringing leftovers back to life, ensuring they're just as crispy and delicious as when first made. Whether it's pizza, chicken, or veggies, skip the microwave and opt for the air fryer to restore the texture and flavor. Just remember to adjust temperature and timing for the best results, and you'll wonder how you ever reheated food any other way.
- **Melted Perfection:** Adding cheese towards the end of cooking in the air fryer is a fantastic way to ensure it melts beautifully without burning. Whether topping a keto pizza, finishing a casserole, or adding richness to vegetables, sprinkle your cheese during the last few minutes. This technique allows the cheese to reach that perfectly gooey texture, elevating your dish with a touch of creamy decadence.
- **Achieving the Crunch:** Want to make your vegetables irresistibly crispy in the air fryer? The key is in the prep. Lightly coat them with a keto-friendly oil, ensure they're not wet from washing, and give them space in the basket for air to circulate freely. Season according to taste before cooking, and consider a sprinkle of parmesan or almond flour for an extra crispy finish.
- **Elevate with Essentials:** To truly master air frying, especially on a keto diet, dive into the world of air fryer accessories. A good meat thermometer ensures your dishes are cooked to perfection, while silicone molds open up a universe of baking possibilities, from muffins to keto-friendly bread. Don't forget about wooden skewers for making easy-to-handle treats and oven gloves to protect your hands from the heat.
- **Go Big with Your Air Fryer:** Cooking for a crowd? Choose an air fryer with a larger capacity to match. A 5 to 6-quart model (or even bigger) is perfect for large families, ensuring you can whip up enough keto-friendly fare for everyone in one go.
- **Double Up for Efficiency:** If your current air fryer doesn't quite meet the demands of your family's size, getting a second one can be a smart move. Cooking different dishes at the same time not only saves you from a logistical headache but also ensures everyone's preferences are catered to efficiently.
- **Air Fryer on the Go:** Your air fryer isn't just for home use; it's also a fantastic companion for trips where you have access to electricity. RVs, vacation rentals, and even tailgating events can be ideal settings to bring along your air fryer.
- **Cooking as Playtime:** Transform cooking time into fun, educational playtime for kids with your air fryer. It's safe, easy, and fast, making it perfect for little chefs to experiment under supervision. Try simple recipes like air-fried cheese sticks, mini pizzas, or even keto-friendly muffins. These activities not only keep them engaged but also teach them about healthy eating habits.

Before we dive into the mouth-watering recipes ahead, I want to remind you that there's a special treat waiting for you in the final chapter. Make sure to check it out for an exclusive bonus that will enhance your keto cooking journey. You won't want to miss it!

Chapter 4:

Breakfast Recipes

Chapter 4 Fotos

4.1 Cheesy Omelet Toast

Yield:
1 serving

Prep time:
5 minutes

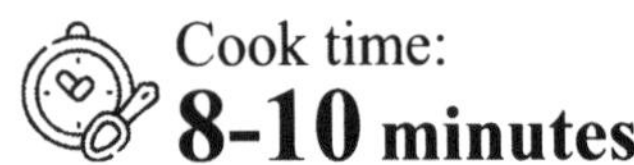
Cook time:
8-10 minutes

Ingredients:

- 1 slice keto bread
- 1 egg, whipped
- 1 tablespoon heavy cream
- 1 teaspoon green onion, diced
- 2 tablespoons mozzarella cheese, shredded
- Pinch of salt
- Dash of pepper
- Precooked bacon bits or diced ham
- Additional mozzarella cheese for topping

Directions:

1. Press the slice of keto bread down in the center, leaving the edges intact. This creates a well to hold the egg mixture. Ensure the bread is placed in the container or the air fryer basket you intend to cook it in before adding the egg mixture.
2. Distribute the precooked bacon bits (or diced ham) and diced green onions evenly across the well in the bread.
3. Sprinkle one layer of shredded mozzarella cheese over the bacon bits and onions.
4. In a bowl, whip the egg with heavy cream, salt, and pepper. Carefully pour this mixture into the bread well. Depending on the egg size, you may need one or two eggs.
5. Add another tablespoon of shredded mozzarella cheese on top of the egg mixture.
6. Bake in the air fryer at 350°F for about 8 to 10 minutes or until the cheese on top is golden brown and fully melted.

Nutritional Information: *Calories: 116 | Carbohydrates: 3.1g | Protein: 13.7g | Fat: 5.7g | Fiber: 1.6g | Sugar: 0.6g*

4.2 Golden Harvest Granola

Yield:
4 servings

Prep time:
5 minutes

Cook time:
8 minutes

Ingredients:

- 1 cup almonds, roughly chopped
- 1/2 cup pecans, roughly chopped
- 1/2 cup shredded unsweetened coconut
- 1/4 cup sunflower seeds
- 1/4 cup pumpkin seeds
- 2 tablespoons chia seeds
- 1/4 cup erythritol (or another keto-friendly sweetener)
- 1 teaspoon cinnamon
- 1/4 teaspoon salt
- 1/4 cup unsalted butter, melted
- 1 teaspoon vanilla extract

Directions:

1. In a large bowl, mix together the almonds, pecans, shredded coconut, sunflower seeds, pumpkin seeds, chia seeds, erythritol, cinnamon, and salt.
2. In a small bowl, whisk together the melted butter and vanilla extract. Pour over the dry ingredients and mix well until everything is evenly coated.
3. Preheat the air fryer to 300°F. Line the air fryer basket with parchment paper or lightly grease it to prevent sticking.
4. Spread the granola mixture evenly in the basket. Air fry for 4 minutes, then stir or shake the basket and continue to air fry for another 4 minutes or until the granola is golden brown and crispy.
5. Let the granola cool completely before serving. It will continue to crisp as it cools.

Nutritional Information: *430 calories, 10g protein, 15g carbohydrates, 40g fat, 9g fiber, 0mg cholesterol, 150mg sodium, 300mg potassium.*

4.3 Cauliflower Crust Egg Muffins

Yield:
6 servings

Prep time:
15 minutes

Cook time:
20 minutes

Ingredients:

- 7 large eggs
- ½ head cauliflower, chopped
- ¼ cup shredded mozzarella cheese (cheddar may be substituted)
- 1 tablespoon sun-dried tomatoes, finely chopped (packed in oil, drained)
- 2 tablespoons grated Parmesan cheese
- ¼ teaspoon garlic powder
- ½ teaspoon onion powder
- Salt and pepper, to taste

Directions:

1. Pulse the cauliflower in a food processor until it reaches a fine, rice-like texture. Microwave the riced cauliflower with the sun-dried tomatoes for about 6-7 minutes until softened. Allow to cool for 4 minutes. If wet, squeeze out the moisture.
2. In a medium-sized bowl, combine the cooled cauliflower mixture, egg white, cheeses, garlic powder, onion powder, salt, and pepper.
3. Spray the muffin tins with cooking oil. Divide the veggie and cheese mixture among 6 muffin cups, pressing the mixture into cup shapes using a shot glass.
4. Preheat the air fryer to 350°F for 5 minutes. Place the muffin tin in the air fryer and cook for 10 minutes. Then, press down any puffiness and crack an egg into each cup. Season with salt and pepper. Air fry at 300°F for 10-12 minutes until the egg whites are set and the yolks are done to your liking.
5. Let cool for a few minutes before removing from the muffin tin. Enjoy your delicious and nutritious egg cups!

Nutritional Information: *112 calories, 9.3g protein, 3.2g carbohydrates, 7.1g fat, 1.2g fiber*

4.4 Spinach and Cheese Egg Muffins

Yield:
1 serving

Prep time:
5 minutes

Cook time:
5-12 minutes

Ingredients:

- 1 large egg
- 1 tablespoon milk or half & half
- 1 tablespoon frozen spinach, thawed (or sautéed fresh spinach)
- 1-2 teaspoons grated cheese (your choice of mozzarella, cheddar, parmesan, feta, goat cheese or spicy pepper jack)
- Salt, to taste
- Black pepper, to taste

Directions:

1. Spray the inside of a silicone muffin cup or ramekin with cooking spray. Place it in the air fryer basket.
2. Add the egg, milk, spinach, and grated cheese into the prepared muffin cup or ramekin. Season with salt and pepper. Gently stir to mix the ingredients without breaking the egg yolk.
3. Set the air fryer to 330°F and cook for about 5-12 minutes. The cooking time will vary based on the number of egg cups being cooked simultaneously and whether you're using a single egg cup or doubling up. Single egg cups typically take about 5 minutes, while multiple or doubled-up cups may take as much as 12 minutes.
4. Cooking in a ceramic ramekin may take a bit longer. If you prefer runny yolks, aim for the shorter end of the cooking range. Keep an eye on the eggs after 5 minutes to achieve your preferred consistency.

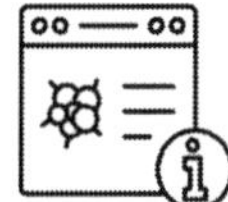

Nutritional Information: *115 calories, 10g protein, 1g carbohydrates, 7g fat, 216mg cholesterol, 173mg sodium, 129mg potassium.*

4.5 Cheesy Ham Omelet Cups

 Yield: **3 servings**

 Prep time: **2 minutes**

 Cook time: **12 minutes**

Ingredients:

- 3 eggs
- 2 oz cream cheese
- ¾ cup diced ham
- ½ cup shredded cheese (your choice of mozzarella, cheddar, etc.)
- ½ teaspoon salt
- ¼ teaspoon pepper

Directions:

1. 1. Set your air fryer to 400°F. Make sure to spray your egg bites mold with cooking spray to prevent sticking.
2. 2. In a blender, combine the eggs with cream cheese, salt, and pepper. Blend until smooth. This ensures that your cream cheese is fully incorporated into the eggs, especially if both are at room temperature.
3. 3. Evenly distribute the diced ham and shredded cheese among the cavities of your egg bites mold. Then, carefully pour the blended egg mixture over the ham and cheese, filling each cavity.
4. 4. Place the mold inside the air fryer. Cook the omelet bites for 10-12 minutes or until they reach an internal temperature of between 165°F and 185°F. After cooking, let them cool for about 5 minutes before popping them out of the mold.

Nutritional Information: *216 calories, 15.9g protein, 2.4g carbohydrates, 15.9g fat, 0.1g fiber, 212.8mg cholesterol, 998mg sodium, 102.1mg potassium.*

4.6 Crispy Bacon and Egg Breakfast Taco

 Yield: **1 serving**

 Prep time: **5 minutes**

 Cook time: **5 minutes**

Ingredients:

- 1 Low Carb or Keto Friendly Tortilla
- 2 tablespoons shredded cheese
- 1 egg
- 4 or 5 strips of precooked bacon, thin-sliced

Directions:

1. Place the tortilla in the air fryer basket. Sprinkle the shredded cheese on the tortilla, leaving a center hole for the egg. The cheese will help to hold the egg in place during cooking.
2. Crack the egg into the center of the cheese on the tortilla. Arrange the precooked bacon slices around the egg on top of the cheese. This placement ensures both the egg and bacon will cook evenly.
3. Set the air fryer to cook at 350°F for exactly 6 minutes. This should be enough time to cook the egg to a soft-medium level and get the edges of the tortilla slightly crispy.
4. Carefully use a fork to lift the edge of the taco to slide it onto your plate. Season with salt and pepper to taste. Allow the taco to cool slightly before eating to avoid any burns from the hot fillings.

Nutritional Information: *325 calories, 28g protein, 3 net carbs, 20g fat, 0g fiber, 185mg cholesterol, 990mg sodium, 200mg potassium.*

4.7 Bacon-Wrapped Egg Delights

Yield:
6 servings

Prep time:
10 minutes

Cook time:
10 minutes

Ingredients:

- 3 slices of bacon, sliced in half
- 6 large eggs
- Diced bell pepper (optional)
- Salt and pepper (optional)

Directions:

1. Slice the bacon strips in half. This will be used to line the muffin cups or silicone baking cups.
2. Line each air fryer cup (either silicone cups sprayed with nonstick cooking spray or paper muffin cups) with a half slice of bacon. This creates a nest for the eggs.
3. Carefully crack an egg into each bacon-lined cup. The bacon acts as a container for the eggs.
4. If desired, sprinkle the tops with diced bell pepper, salt, and pepper to add extra flavor and color.
5. Place the cups in the air fryer basket and cook at 330°F for 10 minutes. The cooking time may vary depending on how you prefer your eggs. For over-medium eggs, start checking at 8 minutes.
6. Once cooked to your liking, carefully remove the egg cups from the air fryer. They will be hot. Garnish with green onions or any other toppings you like.

Nutritional Information: *Calories: 115 kcal | Protein: 8g | Fat: 9g | Fat: 3g | Cholesterol: 210mg | Sodium: 160mg*

4.8 Vanilla Berry Custard Toast

Yield:
2 servings

Prep time:
5 minutes

Cook time:
5 minutes

Ingredients:

- 2 Slices keto bread (your favorite store brand or homemade keto bread)
- ¼ cup plain Greek yogurt
- 2 teaspoons sugar-free honey
- ½ teaspoon vanilla extract
- 1 egg yolk
- 4 strawberries, sliced

Directions:

1. Preheat the air fryer to 350°F and grease a baking dish well.
2. In a medium bowl, add the yogurt, sugar-free honey, vanilla extract, and egg yolk until smooth.
3. Place the bread slices into the greased baking dish. Press down in the center of each piece of bread to form a slight indentation.
4. Pour the yogurt mixture into the indentation of each piece of bread. Add sliced strawberries on top of each slice.
5. Place the prepared bread slices in the air fryer for 5 minutes or until the custard is cooked thoroughly and the bread is toasted to the desired doneness.

Nutritional Information: *Calories: 141, Fat: 4g, Cholesterol: 94mg, Sodium: 167mg, Carbohydrates: 8g, Fiber: 2g, Sugar: 2g, Protein: 7g*

4.9 Cheesy Egg & Bacon Bites

Yield:
4 servings

Prep time:
10 minutes

Cook time:
10 minutes

Ingredients:

- 4 large eggs
- 4 tsp milk
- 1/2 diced onion
- 1/2 small diced bell pepper
- 4 strips of cooked and crumbled bacon
- 1/4 cup shredded cheese
- Salt and pepper to taste

Directions:

1. Place 4 silicone cupcake holders into your air fryer basket.
2. Crack 1 egg into each cup, then add 1 tsp milk into each one. Top each egg with diced onions, green pepper, bacon bits, and cheese. Season with a sprinkle of salt and pepper.
3. Set the air fryer to 300°F and cook for 10-13 minutes or until the egg bites are lightly browned on top and set.
4. Carefully remove the egg bites from the silicone cups and enjoy warm.

Nutritional Information: *195, Fat: 15g, Cholesterol: 186mg, Sodium: 255mg, Potassium: 144mg, Carbohydrates: 3g, Fiber: 1g, Protein: 10g, Calcium: 84mg,*

4.10 Garden Veggie Egg Cups

Yield:
6 servings

Prep time:
10 minutes

Cook time:
9 minutes

Ingredients:

- 6 large eggs
- 2 tablespoons heavy cream
- 1 teaspoon kosher salt
- 1/2 teaspoon black pepper
- 1/4 cup bell peppers, diced
- 1/4 cup white onions, diced
- 1/4 cup Cheddar Cheese, shredded
- 1/4 cup Mozzarella Cheese, shredded

Directions:

1. In a small bowl, combine the shredded cheese and diced vegetables.
2. In another bowl, whisk together the eggs, cream, salt, and black pepper.
3. Add the cheese and vegetable mixture to the egg mixture and stir well.
4. Spray your ramekin, muffin cups, or silicone molds with non-stick cooking spray, then pour the egg mixture into them, filling them about 2/3 full.
5. Place them into the air fryer at 320°F for 5-9 minutes.
6. Let cool for a few minutes before removing from the muffin tin. Enjoy your delicious and nutritious egg cups!

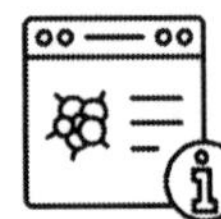

Nutritional Information: *126 calories, 9g protein, 2g carbohydrates, 9g fat, 0.3g fiber, 200mg cholesterol, 521mg sodium, 106mg potassium.*

4.11 Hearty Breakfast Frittata

 Yield: **4 servings**

 Prep time: **10 minutes**

 Cook time: **16 minutes**

Ingredients:

- 4 eggs
- 3 tablespoons heavy cream
- 4 tablespoons grated cheddar cheese
- 4 mushrooms, sliced
- 6 grape tomatoes, halved
- 4 tablespoons chopped spinach
- 2 tablespoons fresh chopped herbs of choice
- 1 green onion, sliced
- Salt to taste

Directions:

1. Preheat the air fryer to 350°F.
2. Line a deep 7-inch baking pan with parchment paper, then oil the pan and set it aside.
3. In a bowl, whisk together the eggs and cream.
4. Add the rest of the ingredients to the bowl, including salt, and stir to combine.
5. Pour the breakfast frittata mixture into the baking pan and place it inside the air fryer basket.
6. Cook for 12-16 minutes or until eggs are set. To check, insert a toothpick in the center of the air fryer frittata. The eggs are set if it comes out clean.

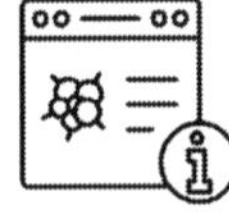

Nutritional Information: *147 calories, 9g protein, 3g carbohydrates, 11g fat, 1g fiber, 188mg cholesterol, 133mg sodium, 237mg potassium.*

4.12 Spicy Breakfast Poblano Boats

 Yield: **2 servings**

 Prep time: **5 minutes**

 Cook time: **13 minutes**

Ingredients:

- 2 poblano peppers, halved, seeds removed
- 4 eggs
- 1 tsp olive oil
- Salt and pepper to taste
- Optional: a pinch of Sriracha flakes for heat

Directions:

1. Preheat the air fryer for 5 minutes.
2. Rub a bit of olive oil on the exposed edges of the halved poblano peppers.
3. Crack two eggs into each bell pepper half. Season with salt, pepper, and Sriracha flakes if desired.
4. Place the stuffed peppers in the air fryer basket.
5. Close the air fryer lid and cook at 390°F for 13 minutes.
6. Once done, remove from the air fryer and serve hot.

Nutritional Information: *164 calories, 11g protein, 4g carbohydrates, 10g fat, 1g fiber, 327mg cholesterol, 146mg sodium, 246mg potassium.*

4.13 Cheesy Avocado Egg Nests

Yield:
4 servings

Prep time:
5 minutes

Cook time:
15 minutes

Ingredients:

- 4 avocados, halved and pitted
- 8 eggs
- Salt and pepper to taste
- 1/4 cup shredded cheddar cheese (optional for topping)
- 2 tablespoons chopped fresh chives (for garnish)

Directions:

1. Preheat your air fryer to 350°F.
2. Scoop out a little extra avocado from the halves to make room for the eggs. Place the avocado halves in the air fryer basket, careful to keep them steady.
3. Crack an egg into each avocado half. Season with salt and pepper. If using, sprinkle the shredded cheddar cheese over each egg.
4. Air fry for about 12-15 minutes or until the eggs are cooked to your liking.
5. Carefully remove the avocado eggs from the air fryer, garnish with chopped chives, and serve immediately.

Nutritional Information: *320 calories, 12g protein, 9g carbohydrates, 29g fat, 7g fiber, 327mg cholesterol, 117mg sodium, 727mg potassium.*

4.14 Sausage and Cheddar Breakfast Muffins

Yield:
6 servings

Prep time:
10 minutes

Cook time:
20 minutes

Ingredients:

- 1 pound ground breakfast sausage
- 1 cup almond flour
- 1/2 cup coconut flour
- 1 tablespoon baking powder
- 4 large eggs
- 1/2 cup sour cream
- 1/4 cup melted butter
- 1 1/2 cups shredded cheddar cheese
- Salt and pepper to taste

Directions:

1. Preheat your oven to 350°F and grease a muffin tin or line with muffin cups.
2. In a skillet over medium heat, cook the sausage until browned and crumbled. Drain any excess fat and set aside to cool slightly.
3. In a large bowl, whisk together almond flour, coconut flour, and baking powder. Add eggs, sour cream, melted butter, salt, and pepper, mixing until well combined. Fold in the cooked sausage and shredded cheese.
4. Divide the mixture evenly among the prepared muffin cups, filling each about three-quarters full.
5. Bake for 20-25 minutes or until the tops are golden brown and a toothpick inserted into the center of a bite comes out clean.
6. Allow cooling for a few minutes before serving.

Nutritional Information: *467 calories, 23g protein, 9g carbohydrates, 38g fat, 4g fiber, 217mg cholesterol, 709mg sodium, 239mg potassium.*

4.15 Crispy Radish Hash Browns

Yield:
4 servings

Prep time:
10 minutes

Cook time:
15 minutes

Ingredients:

- 1 pound radishes, trimmed and grated
- 1/2 medium onion, finely chopped
- 1 clove garlic, minced
- 2 tablespoons olive oil
- Salt and pepper to taste
- 1/4 teaspoon paprika (optional for extra flavor)
- 1/4 cup grated Parmesan cheese (optional for extra crispiness)

Directions:

1. Rinse the grated radishes under cold water and then squeeze out as much liquid as possible using a clean kitchen towel or cheesecloth.
2. In a bowl, mix together the squeezed radishes, chopped onion, minced garlic, olive oil, salt, pepper, and paprika (if using) until well combined. If using Parmesan, fold it into the mixture for added flavor and crispiness.
3. Preheat the air fryer to 390°F. Divide the radish mixture into four equal portions and form each into a patty.
4. Place the patties in the air fryer basket, ensuring they are not touching. Air fry for 12-15 minutes, flipping halfway through, until they are golden brown and crispy.
5. Serve immediately with your favorite low-carb toppings or as a side to your main dish.

Nutritional Information: *76 calories, 2g protein, 4g carbohydrates, 6g fat, 2g fiber, 0mg cholesterol, 87mg sodium, 270mg potassium.m.*

4.16 Savory Scotch Delights

Yield:
4 servings

Prep time:
15 minutes

Cook time:
20 minutes

Ingredients:

- 8 medium eggs (6 for boiling, 2 for dipping)
- 1 pound ground pork sausage
- 1 teaspoon salt
- 1/2 teaspoon black pepper
- 1 teaspoon garlic powder
- 1 teaspoon onion powder
- 1 cup almond flour
- 1 tablespoon dried parsley (optional, for seasoning)

Directions:

1. Start by hard boiling 6 eggs. Place eggs in a pot, cover with water, and bring to a boil. Once boiling, cover the pot with a lid, turn off the heat, and let sit for 9-10 minutes. Then, transfer the eggs to an ice bath to cool.
2. In a bowl, mix the ground pork sausage with salt, pepper, garlic powder, onion powder, and parsley (if using). Divide the sausage mixture into 6 equal portions.
3. Peel the cooled boiled eggs. Wrap each egg evenly with the sausage mixture, making sure the egg is fully covered.
4. Beat the remaining 2 eggs in a bowl. Dip each sausage-wrapped egg into the beaten egg, then roll in almond flour to coat.
5. Preheat the air fryer to 400°F. Place the Scotch eggs in the air fryer basket and spray lightly with oil. Air fry for about 20 minutes, turning halfway through cooking, until the sausage is fully cooked and the exterior is golden brown.
6. Let the Scotch eggs cool slightly before serving. They can be enjoyed warm or at room temperature.

Nutritional Information: *630 calories, 38g protein, 4g carbohydrates, 52g fat, 2g fiber, 372mg cholesterol, 1280mg sodium, 340mg potassium.*

4.17 Almond Flour Pancake Poppers

Yield:
4 servings

Prep time:
10 minutes

Cook time:
10 minutes

Ingredients:

- 1 cup almond flour
- 1/4 cup coconut flour
- 2 tablespoons erythritol (or another keto-friendly sweetener)
- 1 teaspoon baking powder
- 1/4 teaspoon salt
- 4 large eggs
- 1/4 cup unsweetened almond milk
- 2 tablespoons unsalted butter, melted
- 1 teaspoon vanilla extract

Directions:

1. In a mixing bowl, whisk together almond flour, coconut flour, erythritol, baking powder, and salt.
2. In another bowl, beat the eggs, then mix in almond milk, melted butter, and vanilla extract until well combined.
3. Pour the wet ingredients into the dry ingredients and stir until a smooth batter forms.
4. Preheat the air fryer to 350°F. Lightly grease a silicone muffin mold or individual silicone muffin cups with oil.
5. Fill each muffin cup about three-quarters full with the pancake batter.
6. Place the mold or cups in the air fryer basket and cook for about 10 minutes or until the pancake bites are golden brown and a toothpick inserted into the center comes out clean.

Nutritional Information: *295 calories, 12g protein, 10g carbohydrates, 23g fat, 6g fiber, 220mg cholesterol, 310mg sodium, 100mg potassium.*

4.18 Cinnamon Toast Sticks

Yield:
4 servings

Prep time:
15 minutes

Cook time:
10 minutes

Ingredients:

- 1 loaf keto bread (cut into sticks)
- 4 large eggs
- 1/2 cup heavy cream
- 1/4 cup unsweetened almond milk
- 2 tablespoons erythritol
- 1 teaspoon cinnamon
- 1 teaspoon vanilla extract

Directions:

1. 1. In a shallow dish, whisk together the eggs, heavy cream, almond milk, erythritol, cinnamon, and vanilla extract until well combined.
2. 2. Preheat the air fryer to 350°F. Meanwhile, dip each breadstick into the egg mixture, allowing the excess to drip off.
3. 3. Place dipped bread sticks in a single layer in the air fryer basket, ensuring they are not touching. Spray lightly with oil.
4. 4. Air fry for 8-10 minutes, flipping halfway through until the French toast sticks are golden brown and crispy.
5. 5. Serve immediately with keto-friendly syrup or a dusting of erythritol and additional cinnamon if desired.

Nutritional Information: *290 calories, 12g protein, 8g carbohydrates, 24g fat, 5g fiber, 215mg cholesterol, 350mg sodium, 130mg potassium.*

4.19 Mediterranean Bliss Frittata

 Yield: **4 servings**

 Prep time: **5 minutes**

 Cook time: **15 minutes**

Ingredients:

- 6 large eggs
- 1/2 cup heavy cream
- 1/2 teaspoon salt
- 1/4 teaspoon black pepper
- 1 cup fresh spinach, chopped
- 1/2 cup feta cheese, crumbled
- 1/4 cup red onion, finely chopped
- 1 tablespoon olive oil

Directions:

1. In a large bowl, whisk together the eggs, heavy cream, salt, and pepper until well combined.
2. Stir in the chopped spinach, crumbled feta cheese, and red onion.
3. Grease a 7-inch round baking dish or a pan that fits your air fryer with olive oil. Pour the egg mixture into the greased dish.
4. Preheat the air fryer to 360°F. Place the dish in the air fryer basket and cook for 15 minutes or until the frittata is set and lightly golden on top.
5. Allow the frittata to cool for a few minutes before slicing and serving.

Nutritional Information: *290 calories, 14g protein, 4g carbohydrates, 25g fat, 1g fiber, 350mg cholesterol, 670mg sodium, 200mg potassium.*

• •

4.20 Crispy Cauliflower Patties

 Yield: **4 servings**

 Prep time: **15 minutes**

 Cook time: **15 minutes**

Ingredients:

- 1 medium cauliflower, riced (about 4 cups)
- 1/2 cup almond flour
- 1/4 cup grated Parmesan cheese
- 2 large eggs, beaten
- 1/2 teaspoon garlic powder
- 1/2 teaspoon onion powder
- Salt and pepper to taste

Directions:

1. Microwave the riced cauliflower for about 5 minutes or until soft. Allow to cool slightly, then squeeze out as much water as possible using a clean kitchen towel or cheesecloth.
2. In a large bowl, combine the dried cauliflower rice, almond flour, grated Parmesan, beaten eggs, garlic powder, onion powder, salt, and pepper. Mix until well combined.
3. Form the mixture into patties about 4 inches in diameter.
4. Preheat the air fryer to 400°F. Spray the air fryer basket with oil to prevent sticking.
5. Place the hash brown patties in the basket, not touching, and spray the tops lightly with oil. Cook for about 15 minutes, flipping halfway through or until golden brown and crispy.
6. Serve immediately with your favorite low-carb sauce or as a side dish.

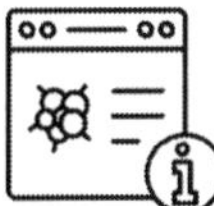

Nutritional Information: *190 calories, 11g protein, 12g carbohydrates, 12g fat, 5g fiber, 94mg cholesterol, 320mg sodium, 430mg potassium.*

4.21 Crispy Bacon Avocado Quarters

Yield:
4 servings

Prep time:
10 minutes

Cook time:
15 minutes

Ingredients:

- 2 ripe avocados, halved and pitted
- 8 slices of bacon
- Salt and pepper to taste
- Optional: chili powder or your favorite seasoning for extra flavor

Directions:

1. Cut each avocado half into 2 quarters, creating 8 pieces in total. Season the avocado pieces with salt, pepper, and optional chili powder or other seasonings.
2. Wrap each avocado quarter with a slice of bacon, ensuring the bacon covers most of the avocado. If necessary, secure the bacon with a toothpick.
3. Preheat the air fryer to 390°F. Place the bacon-wrapped avocado pieces in the air fryer basket, making sure they don't touch.
4. Cook for 12-15 minutes or until the bacon is crispy and golden brown. Halfway through cooking, flip the avocado pieces to ensure even crispiness.
5. Carefully remove the bacon-wrapped avocado from the air fryer and serve immediately.

Nutritional Information: *330 calories, 10g protein, 9g carbohydrates, 30g fat, 7g fiber, 25mg cholesterol, 400mg sodium, 487mg potassium.*

4.22 Mushroom and Swiss Cheese Delight Omelet

Yield:
2 servings

Prep time:
5 minutes

Cook time:
15 minutes

Ingredients:

- 4 large eggs
- 1/4 cup heavy cream
- Salt and pepper to taste
- 1/2 cup sliced mushrooms
- 1/2 cup shredded Swiss cheese
- 1 tablespoon unsalted butter
- 2 tablespoons chopped fresh parsley (optional for garnish)

Directions:

1. In a medium bowl, whisk together the eggs, heavy cream, salt, and pepper until well combined.
2. Melt the butter in the air fryer pan (if compatible) or a small, oven-safe dish that fits in your air fryer basket. Add the mushrooms and cook at 350°F for 5 minutes or until they are softened.
3. Pour the egg mixture over the mushrooms and sprinkle the shredded Swiss cheese on top. Return the pan or dish to the air fryer.
4. Cook at 350°F (175°C) for 10 minutes or until the eggs are set and the cheese is melted and lightly browned.
5. Carefully remove the omelet from the air fryer, garnish with fresh parsley if desired, and serve immediately.

Nutritional Information: *390 calories, 25g protein, 3g carbohydrates, 31g fat, 0g fiber, 450mg cholesterol, 340mg sodium, 200mg potassium.*

4.23 Spring Asparagus with Egg Halves

Yield:
4 servings

Prep time:
5 minutes

Cook time:
15 minutes

Ingredients:

- 1 pound asparagus, ends trimmed
- 4 large eggs
- 2 tablespoons olive oil
- Salt and pepper to taste
- 1 teaspoon garlic powder
- 1 tablespoon grated Parmesan cheese (optional for garnish)
- 1 teaspoon lemon zest (optional for garnish)

Directions:

1. Preheat the air fryer to 400°F. In a bowl, toss the asparagus with olive oil, salt, pepper, and garlic powder until evenly coated.
2. Place the asparagus in the air fryer basket in a single layer. Cook for 7-10 minutes or until tender and slightly crispy, shaking the basket halfway through.
3. While the asparagus cooks, bring a pot of water to a boil. Carefully add the eggs and cook for 6-7 minutes for soft-boiled eggs. Remove eggs and place in an ice bath to stop the cooking process. Once cooled, peel the eggs.
4. Arrange the cooked asparagus on a plate. Cut the soft-boiled eggs in half and place on top of the asparagus. Season with additional salt and pepper if desired. Garnish with grated Parmesan cheese and lemon zest if using.
5. Serve immediately for a warm, nutritious meal.

Nutritional Information: *Information: 184 calories, 10g protein, 6g carbohydrates, 14g fat, 3g fiber, 186mg cholesterol, 200mg sodium, 370mg potassium.*

Chapter 5:

Quick & Easy Recipes for Everyday

5.1 Aromatic Spiced Chicken Delight

Yield:
4 servings

Prep time:
10 minutes

Cook time:
20 minutes

Ingredients:

- 4 bone-in, skin-on chicken thighs
- 1 tablespoon olive oil
- 1 teaspoon garlic powder
- 1 teaspoon paprika
- 1 teaspoon dried thyme
- Salt and pepper to taste

Directions:

1. Preheat the air fryer to 375°F.
2. In a small bowl, mix together olive oil, garlic powder, paprika, dried thyme, salt, and pepper.
3. Pat the chicken thighs dry with paper towels and rub the seasoning mixture all over them.
4. Place the seasoned chicken thighs in the air fryer basket, skin side down, and cook for 10 minutes. Flip the chicken thighs and cook for an additional 10 minutes or until the internal temperature reaches 165°F (75°C) and the skin is crispy.

Nutritional Information: *310 calories, 24g protein, 0g carbohydrates, 24g fat, 0g fiber, 130mg cholesterol, 380mg sodium, 240mg potassium.*

5.2 Smoky Paprika Shrimp Sensation

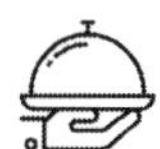
Yield:
4 servings

Prep time:
10 minutes

Cook time:
8 minutes

Ingredients:

- 1 pound large shrimp, peeled and deveined
- 1 tablespoon olive oil
- 1 teaspoon garlic powder
- 1 teaspoon smoked paprika
- 1/2 teaspoon salt
- 1/4 teaspoon black pepper
- Lemon wedges for serving (optional)

Directions:

1. In a large bowl, toss the shrimp with olive oil, garlic powder, smoked paprika, salt, and black pepper until well coated.
2. Preheat the air fryer to 400°F. Arrange the shrimp in a single layer in the air fryer basket. You may need to work in batches depending on the size of your air fryer.
3. Cook for 8 minutes, shaking the basket halfway through or until the shrimp are golden and cooked through.
4. Serve immediately with lemon wedges on the side if desired.

Nutritional Information: *120 calories, 24g protein, 1g carbohydrates, 2g fat, 0g fiber, 182mg cholesterol, 879mg sodium, 220mg potassium.*

5.3 Crispy Almond-Crusted Mozzarella Bites

 Yield: **4 servings**

 Prep time: **15 minutes**

 Cook time: **5 minutes**

Ingredients:

- 8 mozzarella string cheese sticks, cut in half
- 1 cup almond flour
- 1 tablespoon Italian seasoning
- 1/2 teaspoon garlic powder
- 1/2 teaspoon salt
- 2 large eggs, beaten
- 1/2 cup grated Parmesan cheese

Directions:

1. Freeze the mozzarella sticks for at least 1 hour or until completely solid.
2. In a shallow bowl, mix the almond flour, Italian seasoning, garlic powder, and salt. In another shallow bowl, beat the eggs. In a third shallow bowl, place the grated Parmesan cheese.
3. Dip each frozen mozzarella stick first in the egg, then in the almond flour mixture, back in the egg, and finally coat it with the Parmesan cheese. Make sure each stick is well coated at each step.
4. Preheat the air fryer to 400°F. Place the coated mozzarella sticks in a single layer in the basket. Work in batches if necessary to avoid overcrowding.
5. Cook for 5 minutes or until golden and crispy. Serve immediately.

Nutritional Information: *320 calories, 21g protein, 5g carbohydrates, 24g fat, 2g fiber, 85mg cholesterol, 670mg sodium, 90mg potassium.*

5.4 Spicy Buffalo Cauliflower Poppers

 Yield: **4 servings**

 Prep time: **10 minutes**

 Cook time: **20 minutes**

Ingredients:

- 1 head of cauliflower, cut into bite-sized florets
- 1/4 cup olive oil
- 1/2 cup buffalo sauce (make sure it's low-carb)
- 1 teaspoon garlic powder
- 1 teaspoon paprika
- Salt and pepper to taste
- Optional: Blue cheese or ranch dressing for serving

Directions:

1. In a large bowl, combine the olive oil, buffalo sauce, garlic powder, paprika, salt, and pepper. Add the cauliflower florets and toss until they are evenly coated with the sauce mixture.
2. Preheat the air fryer to 400°F. Place the cauliflower florets in the air fryer basket in a single layer, ensuring they are not overcrowded. You may need to cook them in batches, depending on the size of your air fryer.
3. Cook for 20 minutes, shaking the basket halfway through the cooking time or until the cauliflower is crispy and has a nice golden color.
4. Serve hot with blue cheese or ranch dressing on the side, if desired.

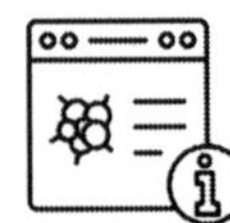

Nutritional Information: *125 calories, 2g protein, 5g carbohydrates, 10g fat, 2g fiber, 0mg cholesterol, 1075mg sodium, 320mg potassium.*

5.5 Herb-Infused Salmon Patties

Yield:
4 servings

Prep time:
15 minutes

Cook time:
10 minutes

Ingredients:

- 2 cans (6 ounces each) salmon, drained and flaked
- 1/2 cup almond flour
- 2 large eggs, beaten
- 2 tablespoons mayonnaise
- 2 tablespoons fresh dill, chopped (or 2 teaspoons dried dill)
- 1 teaspoon garlic powder
- 1 teaspoon onion powder
- Salt and pepper to taste
- 2 tablespoons olive oil for brushing
- Lemon wedges for serving

Directions:

1. In a large bowl, combine the flaked salmon, almond flour, eggs, mayonnaise, dill, garlic powder, onion powder, salt, and pepper. Mix well until the mixture is homogeneous.
2. Form the mixture into 8 equal-sized patties. If the mixture is too sticky, you can slightly wet your hands with water to make handling easier.
3. Preheat the air fryer to 400°F. Brush both sides of the salmon patties with olive oil to prevent sticking and to help them get a golden color.
4. Place the salmon patties in the air fryer basket in a single layer, ensuring they do not touch. You may need to cook them in batches, depending on the size of your air fryer.
5. Cook for 10 minutes, flipping the patties halfway through or until they are golden brown and cooked through.
6. Serve hot with lemon wedges on the side.

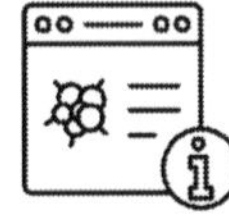

Nutritional Information: *230 calories, 23g protein, 3g carbohydrates, 14g fat, 2g fiber, 105mg cholesterol, 390mg sodium, 290mg potassium.*

5.6 Cheesy Stuffed Jalapenos

Yield:
4 servings

Prep time:
15 minutes

Cook time:
10 minutes

Ingredients:

- 8 jalapenos, halved and seeded
- 1 cup cream cheese, softened
- 1/2 cup shredded cheddar cheese
- 1/4 cup grated Parmesan cheese
- 1/4 teaspoon garlic powder
- 1/4 teaspoon onion powder
- 1/4 teaspoon paprika
- 1/2 cup almond flour
- 1 large egg, beaten
- 1 cup crushed pork rinds

Directions:

1. In a bowl, mix together the cream cheese, cheddar cheese, Parmesan cheese, garlic powder, onion powder, and paprika until well combined. Stuff each jalapeno half with the cheese mixture.
2. Prepare two shallow dishes: one with beaten egg and another with a mixture of almond flour and crushed pork rinds. Dip each stuffed jalapeno first into the egg, then coat with the almond flour and pork rinds mixture.
3. Place the coated jalapenos in the air fryer basket. Set the air fryer to 390°F and cook for 10 minutes or until the jalapenos are golden and crispy.
4. Serve immediately.

Nutritional Information: *345 calories, 16g protein, 6g carbohydrates, 29g fat, 2g fiber, 90mg cholesterol, 350mg sodium, 250mg potassium.*

5.7 Italian-Style Beef Meatballs

Yield:
4 servings

Prep time:
15 minutes

Cook time:
15 minutes

Ingredients:

- 1 pound ground beef (85% lean)
- 1/4 cup almond flour
- 1 large egg
- 1/4 cup grated Parmesan cheese
- 2 cloves garlic, minced
- 1 teaspoon salt
- 1/2 teaspoon black pepper
- 1/2 teaspoon dried oregano
- 1/4 teaspoon red pepper flakes (optional)

Directions:

1. In a large bowl, combine ground beef, almond flour, egg, Parmesan cheese, garlic, salt, pepper, dried oregano, and red pepper flakes. Mix well until all ingredients are evenly distributed.
2. Form the mixture into meatballs about 1.5 inches in diameter. You should get approximately 16 meatballs.
3. Preheat the air fryer to 400°F. Place meatballs in the air fryer basket, ensuring they are not touching. Cook in batches if necessary.
4. Cook for about 15 minutes or until the meatballs are browned on the outside and no longer pink in the center. Shake the basket halfway through cooking to ensure even browning.

Nutritional Information: *330 calories, 23g protein, 2g carbohydrates, 25g fat, 1g fiber, 105mg cholesterol, 640mg sodium, 340mg potassium.*

5.8 Golden Broccoli Cheese Poppers

Yield:
4 servings

Prep time:
10 minutes

Cook time:
8 minutes

Ingredients:

- 2 cups broccoli florets, finely chopped
- 1 cup shredded cheddar cheese
- 1/3 cup almond flour
- 1 large egg, beaten
- 1/2 teaspoon garlic powder
- 1/2 teaspoon onion powder
- Salt and pepper to taste

Directions:

1. In a large bowl, combine the finely chopped broccoli, shredded cheddar cheese, almond flour, beaten egg, garlic powder, onion powder, salt, and pepper. Mix until all ingredients are well incorporated.
2. Form the mixture into small, bite-sized balls about 1 inch in diameter. You should get around 16-20 bites.
3. Preheat the air fryer to 375°F.
4. Place the broccoli cheese bites in the basket, ensuring they are not touching for proper air circulation. Cook in batches if necessary.
5. Air fry for about 8 minutes or until the bites are golden brown and crispy on the outside. Halfway through cooking, shake the basket or gently turn the bites to ensure even cooking.

Nutritional Information: *160 calories, 10g protein, 4g carbohydrates, 12g fat, 2g fiber, 60mg cholesterol, 200mg sodium, 180mg potassium.*

5.9 Hearty Air-Fried Sausage & Peppers

Yield:
4 servings

Prep time:
10 minutes

Cook time:
12 minutes

Ingredients:

- 4 Italian sausages (pork or turkey, about 1 pound total)
- 2 bell peppers (any color), sliced into strips
- 1 medium onion, sliced
- 1 tablespoon olive oil
- 1/2 teaspoon salt
- 1/4 teaspoon black pepper
- 1/2 teaspoon dried oregano
- 1/4 teaspoon red pepper flakes (optional)

Directions:

1. In a large bowl, toss the sliced bell peppers and onion with olive oil, salt, pepper, dried oregano, and red pepper flakes until they are evenly coated.
2. Place the sausages in the air fryer basket and spread the seasoned peppers and onions around and on top of them.
3. Preheat the air fryer to 400°F. Cook for about 12 minutes or until the sausages are cooked through and the vegetables are tender and slightly charred. Turn the sausages and stir the vegetables halfway through the cooking time.
4. Serve immediately, either on its own for a keto-friendly meal or with a side of your choice.

Nutritional Information: *390 calories, 21g protein, 6g carbohydrates, 31g fat, 1g fiber, 85mg cholesterol, 870mg sodium, 320mg potassium.*

5.10 Parmesan Garlic Chicken Wings

Yield:
4 servings

Prep time:
10 minutes

Cook time:
20 minutes

Ingredients:

- 2 pounds chicken wings, tips removed and wings split at the joint
- 2 tablespoons olive oil
- 1/2 teaspoon salt
- 1/4 teaspoon black pepper
- 4 cloves garlic, minced
- 1/2 cup grated Parmesan cheese
- 1 tablespoon fresh parsley, finely chopped (optional for garnish)

Directions:

1. In a large bowl, toss the chicken wings with olive oil, salt, and black pepper until they are evenly coated.
2. Preheat the air fryer to 400°F. Place the wings in the air fryer basket in a single layer, ensuring they are not touching for optimal airflow. You may need to cook in batches, depending on the size of your air fryer.
3. Cook for about 20 minutes or until the wings are golden brown and crispy, turning them halfway through the cooking time.
4. In the last 5 minutes of cooking, sprinkle the minced garlic over the wings.
5. Once cooked, toss the wings in grated Parmesan cheese and garnish with chopped parsley if desired.
6. Serve immediately, enjoying a crispy, flavorful, and keto-friendly treat.

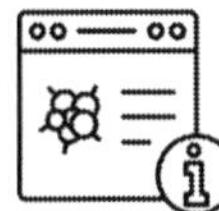

Nutritional Information: *440 calories, 35g protein, 1g carbohydrates, 34g fat, 0g fiber, 150mg cholesterol, 640mg sodium, 300mg potassium.*

5.11 Almond-Crusted Tofu Delights

Yield:
4 servings

Prep time:
15 minutes

Cook time:
15 minutes

Ingredients:

- 1 block (14 ounces) extra-firm tofu, pressed and cubed
- 2 tablespoons soy sauce (or tamari for a gluten-free option)
- 1 tablespoon olive oil
- 1 tablespoon almond flour
- 1 teaspoon garlic powder
- 1/2 teaspoon onion powder
- Salt and pepper to taste

Directions:

1. Press the tofu to remove excess water. Wrap the tofu in paper towels or a clean kitchen towel and place a heavy object on top, such as a skillet or a can. Let it sit for about 10 minutes to press out the water.
2. Cut the pressed tofu into 1-inch cubes.
3. In a large bowl, whisk together soy sauce, olive oil, almond flour, garlic powder, onion powder, salt, and pepper. Add the tofu cubes to the bowl and gently toss to coat them evenly with the seasoning mixture.
4. Preheat the air fryer to 400°F. Arrange the tofu cubes in the air fryer basket in a single layer, ensuring they are not touching for optimal airflow. You may need to cook in batches.
5. Cook for about 15 minutes or until the tofu is golden brown and crispy, shaking the basket or turning the tofu halfway through the cooking time.
6. Serve immediately. Enjoy your keto-friendly crispy tofu as a snack or as part of a meal.

Nutritional Information: *150 calories, 10g protein, 3g carbohydrates, 11g fat, 1g fiber, 0mg cholesterol, 350mg sodium, 200mg potassium.*

• •

5.12 Cheesy Zucchini Bites

Yield:
4 servings

Prep time:
15 minutes

Cook time:
10 minutes

Ingredients:

- 2 medium zucchinis, thinly sliced
- 1 tablespoon olive oil
- 1/2 teaspoon sea salt
- 1/4 teaspoon ground black pepper
- 1/4 teaspoon garlic powder
- 1/4 teaspoon paprika
- 1/2 cup grated Parmesan cheese

Directions:

1. 1. Preheat the air fryer to 375°F. In a large bowl, toss the zucchini slices with olive oil, sea salt, black pepper, garlic powder, and paprika until evenly coated.
2. 2. Arrange zucchini slices in a single layer in the air fryer basket, ensuring they do not overlap. You may need to cook them in batches, depending on the size of your air fryer.
3. 3. Cook for 10 minutes, flipping the zucchini chips halfway through or until they are golden and crispy. Remove from the air fryer and sprinkle with grated Parmesan cheese while still hot.

Nutritional Information: *114 calories, 7g protein, 3g carbohydrates, 9g fat, 1g fiber, 17mg cholesterol, 391mg sodium, 230mg potassium.*

5.13 Mozzarella-Topped Eggplant Rounds

 Yield: **4 servings**

 Prep time: **20 minutes**

 Cook time: **20 minutes**

Ingredients:

- 1 large eggplant, sliced into 1/2-inch thick rounds
- 1 teaspoon sea salt for sweating eggplant
- 2 large eggs
- 1 cup almond flour
- 1/2 cup grated Parmesan cheese
- 1 teaspoon Italian seasoning
- 1/2 teaspoon garlic powder
- 1/4 teaspoon ground black pepper
- 1 cup marinara sauce, low-carb
- 1 cup shredded mozzarella cheese
- Fresh basil leaves for garnish (optional)

Directions:

1. Sprinkle the eggplant slices with sea salt and let them sit for about 10 minutes to sweat out bitterness. Rinse the eggplant slices with water and pat them dry with paper towels.
2. Preheat the air fryer to 375°F. In a shallow bowl, beat the eggs. In another shallow bowl, mix together almond flour, grated Parmesan cheese, Italian seasoning, garlic powder, and black pepper.
3. Dip each eggplant slice first into the egg mixture, then into the almond flour mixture, pressing the coating onto the eggplant to stick.
4. Place the coated eggplant slices in a single layer in the air fryer basket, working in batches if necessary. Cook for 10 minutes, flip, and then cook for another 8-10 minutes or until golden and crispy.
5. Top each eggplant round with marinara sauce and shredded mozzarella cheese. Return to the air fryer and cook for an additional 2 minutes or until the cheese is melted and bubbly.
6. Garnish with fresh basil leaves before serving, if desired.

Nutritional Information: *295 calories, 18g protein, 14g carbohydrates, 20g fat, 7g fiber, 106mg cholesterol, 703mg sodium, 467mg potassium.*

5.14 Savory Chicken Fingers

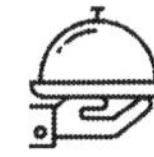 Yield: **4 servings**

Prep time: **15 minutes**

Cook time: **20 minutes**

Ingredients:

- 1 pound chicken breast, cut into strips
- 1 cup almond flour
- 1/2 cup grated Parmesan cheese
- 1 teaspoon paprika
- 1/2 teaspoon garlic powder
- 1/2 teaspoon onion powder
- 1/4 teaspoon salt
- 1/4 teaspoon black pepper
- 2 large eggs, beaten

Directions:

1. Preheat the air fryer to 400°F. In a shallow bowl, combine the almond flour, grated Parmesan cheese, paprika, garlic powder, onion powder, salt, and pepper.
2. Dip each chicken strip into the beaten eggs, then dredge in the almond flour mixture until well coated.
3. Place the coated chicken strips in a single layer in the air fryer basket, ensuring they are not touching. Work in batches if necessary.
4. Cook for 10 minutes, flip the chicken strips, and then cook for an additional 10 minutes or until the chicken is golden brown and reaches an internal temperature of 165°F.
5. Serve immediately.

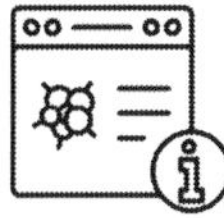

Nutritional Information: *345 calories, 39g protein, 6g carbohydrates, 19g fat, 3g fiber, 162mg cholesterol, 470mg sodium, 320mg potassium.*

Chapter 6:

Appetizers and Snacks

6.1 Savory Mushroom Delights

Yield:
4 servings

Prep time:
15 minutes

Cook time:
10 minutes

Ingredients:

- 12 large cremini or button mushrooms, stems removed
- 4 ounces cream cheese, softened
- 1/4 cup grated Parmesan cheese
- 1/4 cup finely chopped cooked bacon (about 4 slices)
- 1 green onion, finely chopped
- 1 garlic clove, minced
- Salt and pepper, to taste
- 1/4 teaspoon smoked paprika

Directions:

1. In a mixing bowl, combine cream cheese, Parmesan cheese, cooked bacon, green onion, minced garlic, salt, pepper, and smoked paprika. Mix well until all ingredients are evenly incorporated.
2. Fill each mushroom cap with the cream cheese mixture, pressing it in gently to stuff the mushrooms well.
3. Brush the outside of the mushrooms lightly with oil. This helps to keep them moist and adds extra flavor.
4. Preheat the air fryer to 350°F. Arrange the stuffed mushrooms in the air fryer basket in a single layer. Cook for about 10 minutes or until the mushrooms are tender and the filling is golden brown on top.
5. Serve immediately.

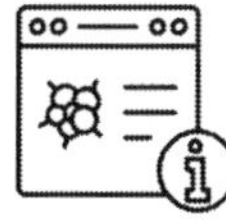
Nutritional Information: *160 calories, 8g protein, 5g carbohydrates, 12g fat, 1g fiber, 30mg cholesterol, 220mg sodium, 350mg potassium.*

6.2 Crispy Pepperoni Chips

Yield:
2 servings

Prep time:
5 minutes

Cook time:
4 minutes

Ingredients:

- 24 slices of pepperoni

Directions:

1. Arrange the pepperoni slices in a single layer in the air fryer basket. If your air fryer is small, you might need to do this in batches to prevent overlap.
2. Cook at 400°F for about 4 minutes or until the pepperoni slices are crispy. Watch closely, as cooking times may vary depending on the air fryer model.
3. Remove the pepperoni chips from the air fryer and place them on a paper towel to drain any excess oil. They will continue to crisp up as they cool.

Nutritional Information: *100 calories, 5g protein, 0g carbohydrates, 9g fat, 0g fiber, 25mg cholesterol, 500mg sodium, 0mg potassium.*

6.3 Savory Cheese Puffs

Yield:
4 servings

Prep time:
10 minutes

Cook time:
5 minutes

Ingredients:

- 1 cup mozzarella cheese, shredded
- 1/2 cup almond flour
- 1/4 cup grated Parmesan cheese
- 1 large egg
- 1 teaspoon garlic powder
- 1 teaspoon Italian seasoning
- Salt to taste

Directions:

1. In a large bowl, mix together the mozzarella cheese, almond flour, grated Parmesan cheese, egg, garlic powder, Italian seasoning, and salt until well combined.
2. Form the mixture into small, bite-sized balls about one inch in diameter.
3. Preheat the air fryer to 400°F. Place the cheese bites in the basket, making sure they are not touching to allow for even cooking.
4. Cook in the air fryer for 5 minutes or until the cheese bites are golden brown and crispy. Shake the basket halfway through the cooking time to ensure they cook evenly.

Nutritional Information: *220 calories, 14g protein, 4g carbohydrates, 17g fat, 2g fiber, 35mg cholesterol, 310mg sodium, 100mg potassium.*

6.4 Avocado Bliss Fingers

Yield:
4 servings

Prep time:
10 minutes

Cook time:
8 minutes

Ingredients:

- 2 large avocados, sliced into wedges
- 1/2 cup almond flour
- 1/4 cup coconut flour
- 1 teaspoon paprika
- 1/2 teaspoon garlic powder
- 1/2 teaspoon onion powder
- Salt and pepper to taste
- 2 large eggs, beaten

Directions:

1. In a shallow dish, combine the almond flour, coconut flour, paprika, garlic powder, onion powder, salt, and pepper.
2. Dip each avocado wedge first into the beaten eggs, then coat with the flour mixture.
3. Preheat the air fryer to 400°F. Place the avocado fries in the air fryer basket in a single layer, ensuring they do not touch for even cooking. You may need to work in batches depending on the size of your air fryer.
4. Cook for 8 minutes or until the avocado fries are golden and crispy. Halfway through the cooking time, gently flip the fries to ensure even cooking.

Nutritional Information: *250 calories, 6g protein, 15g carbohydrates, 20g fat, 10g fiber, 93mg cholesterol, 210mg sodium, 708mg potassium.*

6.5 Fiesta-Style Low-Carb Nachos

Yield: **4 servings**

Prep time: **10 minutes**

Cook time: **5 minutes**

Ingredients:

- 2 cups low-carb tortilla chips, homemade or store-bought
- 1 cup shredded cheddar cheese
- 1/2 cup cooked and shredded chicken
- 1/4 cup sliced jalapenos
- 1/4 cup diced tomatoes
- 1/4 cup sliced black olives
- 1/4 cup diced red onions
- 1/4 cup sour cream for serving
- 1/4 cup guacamole, for serving
- Fresh cilantro, chopped, for garnish

Directions:

1. Arrange the low-carb tortilla chips in the bottom of the air fryer basket. Try to keep them in a single layer for even cooking.
2. Evenly distribute the shredded chicken over the chips, followed by the shredded cheddar cheese.
3. Sprinkle the sliced jalapenos, diced tomatoes, sliced black olives, and diced red onions over the top.
4. Preheat the air fryer to 350°F. Insert the basket and cook for about 5 minutes or until the cheese is melted and bubbly.
5. Carefully remove the nachos from the air fryer. Top with dollops of sour cream and guacamole before serving. Garnish with chopped fresh cilantro.

Nutritional Information: *300 calories, 18g protein, 10g carbohydrates, 20g fat, 5g fiber, 50mg cholesterol, 500mg sodium, 200mg potassium.*

6.6 Almond Parmesan Pickle Bites

Yield: **4 servings**

Prep time: **15 minutes**

Cook time: **8 minutes**

Ingredients:

- 1 cup dill pickle slices, drained and patted dry
- 1/2 cup almond flour
- 1/4 cup grated Parmesan cheese
- 1 teaspoon garlic powder
- 1/2 teaspoon paprika
- Salt and pepper to taste
- 1 large egg
- 1 tablespoon water

Directions:

1. In a small bowl, whisk together the egg and water until well combined.
2. In another bowl, mix the almond flour, grated Parmesan cheese, garlic powder, paprika, salt, and pepper.
3. Dip each pickle slice into the egg mixture, then dredge in the almond flour mixture, making sure the pickle is fully coated.
4. Preheat the air fryer to 400°F. Place the coated pickle slices in the air fryer basket in a single layer, ensuring they do not touch for even cooking.
5. Cook in the air fryer for 8 minutes or until the pickles are golden and crispy. You may need to do this in batches, depending on the size of your air fryer.
6. Serve immediately.

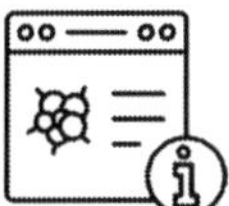

Nutritional Information: *150 calories, 8g protein, 6g carbohydrates, 10g fat, 3g fiber, 55mg cholesterol, 870mg sodium, 200mg potassium.*

6.7 Coconut Bliss Shrimp

Yield: **4 servings**

Prep time: **15 minutes**

Cook time: **10 minutes**

Ingredients:

- 1 pound large shrimp, peeled and deveined, tails left on
- 1/2 cup coconut flour
- 1 teaspoon garlic powder
- 1/2 teaspoon paprika
- Salt and pepper to taste
- 2 large eggs
- 1 cup unsweetened shredded coconut

Directions:

1. In a shallow bowl, combine the coconut flour, garlic powder, paprika, salt, and pepper.
2. In another shallow bowl, beat the eggs.
3. Dip each shrimp first into the coconut flour mixture, then into the beaten eggs, and finally coat it with the shredded coconut.
4. Preheat the air fryer to 400°F.
5. Place the coated shrimp in the air fryer basket in a single layer, making sure they do not touch for even cooking. You may need to cook in batches, depending on the size of your air fryer.
6. Cook for 10 minutes or until the shrimp are golden and cooked through. Flip halfway through the cooking time to ensure even browning.
7. Serve immediately.

Nutritional Information: *280 calories, 25g protein, 10g carbohydrates, 15g fat, 7g fiber, 220mg cholesterol, 300mg sodium, 200mg potassium.*

6.8 Smoked Paprika Radish Snacks

Yield: **4 servings**

Prep time: **10 minutes**

Cook time: **10 minutes**

Ingredients:

- 2 cups radishes, thinly sliced
- 1 tablespoon olive oil
- 1 teaspoon garlic powder
- 1 teaspoon smoked paprika
- Salt and pepper to taste

Directions:

1. In a large bowl, toss the thinly sliced radishes with olive oil, garlic powder, smoked paprika, salt, and pepper until well coated.
2. Preheat the air fryer to 400°F. Arrange the radish slices in a single layer in the air fryer basket, ensuring they do not overlap for even cooking. You may need to work in batches depending on the size of your air fryer.
3. Cook for 10 minutes or until the radish chips are crispy and lightly browned, flipping halfway through the cooking time.
4. Serve immediately as a snack or side dish.

Nutritional Information: *50 calories, 1g protein, 4g carbohydrates, 3.5g fat, 1.5g fiber, 0mg cholesterol, 45mg sodium, 270mg potassium.*

6.9 Parmesan Bean Spears

Yield:
4 servings

Prep time:
15 minutes

Cook time:
10 minutes

Ingredients:

- 1 pound fresh green beans, trimmed
- 1 cup almond flour
- 1/2 cup grated Parmesan cheese
- 1 teaspoon garlic powder
- 1/2 teaspoon onion powder
- Salt and pepper to taste
- 2 large eggs, beaten

Directions:

1. In a shallow bowl, mix together the almond flour, grated Parmesan cheese, garlic powder, onion powder, salt, and pepper.
2. Dip each green bean into the beaten eggs, then coat it with the almond flour mixture.
3. Preheat the air fryer to 400°F.
4. Arrange the coated green beans in a single layer in the air fryer basket, ensuring they do not touch for even cooking. You may need to cook in batches, depending on the size of your air fryer.
5. Cook for 10 minutes or until the green beans are golden and crispy. Shake the basket halfway through the cooking time to ensure even cooking.
6. Serve immediately.

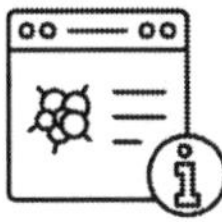
Nutritional Information: *220 calories, 14g protein, 10g carbohydrates, 15g fat, 6g fiber, 110mg cholesterol, 300mg sodium, 400mg potassium.*

6.10 Cauliflower Nuggets

Yield:
4 servings

Prep time:
20 minutes

Cook time:
15 minutes

Ingredients:

- 1 medium head of cauliflower, cut into florets
- 1 cup almond flour
- 1/2 cup grated Parmesan cheese
- 1 teaspoon garlic powder
- 1 teaspoon onion powder
- Salt and pepper to taste
- 2 large eggs, beaten

Directions:

1. Steam the cauliflower florets until tender, about 5-7 minutes. Allow them to cool slightly, then finely chop them or pulse a few times in a food processor until they resemble coarse crumbs.
2. Transfer the chopped cauliflower to a large bowl. Add the almond flour, grated Parmesan cheese, garlic powder, onion powder, salt, and pepper. Mix well to combine.
3. Stir in the beaten eggs until the mixture is well combined and sticks together.
4. Form the mixture into small tot shapes, about 1 inch in length.
5. Preheat the air fryer to 400°F.
6. Place the cauliflower tots in the basket, making sure they do not touch for even cooking. You may need to cook in batches, depending on the size of your air fryer.
7. Cook for 15 minutes or until the tots are golden brown and crispy, turning them halfway through the cooking time.
8. Serve immediately.

Nutritional Information: *220 calories, 14g protein, 10g carbohydrates, 16g fat, 5g fiber, 110mg cholesterol, 320mg sodium, 430mg potassium.*

6.11 Bell Pepper Chicken Nachos

Yield:
4 servings

Prep time:
15 minutes

Cook time:
10 minutes

Ingredients:

- 1 pound mini bell peppers, halved and seeds removed
- 1 cup cooked and shredded chicken
- 1/2 cup shredded cheddar cheese
- 1/4 cup diced red onion
- 1/4 cup sliced black olives
- 1/4 cup diced tomatoes
- 1 avocado, diced
- 1/4 cup sour cream for garnish
- 1 jalapeno, sliced for garnish
- Fresh cilantro, chopped for garnish
- Salt and pepper to taste

Directions:

1. Preheat your air fryer to 375°F. Arrange the halved mini bell peppers in a single layer in the air fryer basket. You may need to do this in batches, depending on the size of your air fryer.
2. Sprinkle the shredded chicken evenly over the bell peppers, followed by the shredded cheddar cheese, red onion, black olives, and diced tomatoes.
3. Cook in the air fryer for about 10 minutes or until the cheese is melted and bubbly.
4. Once cooked, carefully remove the mini bell pepper nachos from the air fryer. Garnish with diced avocado, sour cream, jalapeno slices, and fresh cilantro.
5. Season with salt and pepper to taste before serving.

Nutritional Information: *280 calories, 18g protein, 12g carbohydrates, 20g fat, 5g fiber, 55mg cholesterol, 320mg sodium, 640mg potassium.*

6.12 Buffalo Chicken Creamy Delight

Yield:
4 servings

Prep time:
10 minutes

Cook time:
20 minutes

Ingredients:

- 2 cups cooked chicken, shredded
- 1/2 cup buffalo sauce
- 1/2 cup cream cheese, softened
- 1/4 cup sour cream
- 1/2 cup shredded cheddar cheese
- 1/4 cup crumbled blue cheese (optional)
- 1/4 cup green onions, chopped for garnish

Directions:

1. In a mixing bowl, combine the shredded chicken and buffalo sauce. Stir until the chicken is well-coated.
2. Add the cream cheese and sour cream to the chicken mixture. Mix until well combined.
3. Transfer the mixture into an air fryer-safe dish. Sprinkle the top with cheddar cheese and blue cheese (if using).
4. Place the dish in the air fryer and cook at 350°F for 15-20 minutes or until the cheese is melted and slightly golden.
5. Garnish with chopped green onions before serving.

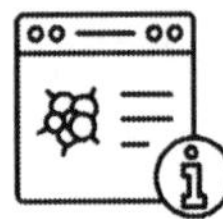

Nutritional Information: *350 calories, 25g protein, 3g carbohydrates, 26g fat, 0g fiber, 85mg cholesterol, 1200mg sodium, 200mg potassium.*

6.13 Cheesy Halloumi Sticks

Yield:
4 servings

Prep time:
5 minutes

Cook time:
10 minutes

Ingredients:

- 8 oz halloumi cheese, cut into 1/2-inch thick fries
- 1 tablespoon avocado oil
- 1 teaspoon paprika (optional for added flavor)
- 1/4 teaspoon garlic powder (optional for added flavor)

Directions:

1. Preheat the air fryer to 400°F.
2. In a bowl, toss the halloumi fries with avocado oil, paprika, and garlic powder until well coated.
3. Arrange the halloumi fries in a single layer in the air fryer basket, ensuring they do not overlap.
4. Cook for 10 minutes, flipping halfway through or until the fries are golden brown and crispy.
5. Serve immediately.

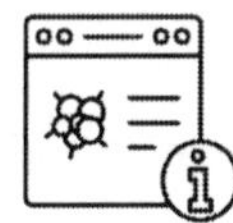

Nutritional Information: *300 calories, 18g protein, 2g carbohydrates, 24g fat, 0g fiber, 50mg cholesterol, 900mg sodium, 100mg potassium.*

6.14 Almond-Crusted Zucchini Medallions

Yield:
4 servings

Prep time:
15 minutes

Cook time:
10 minutes

Ingredients:

- 2 medium zucchinis, cut into 1/2-inch thick rounds
- 1/4 cup almond flour
- 1/4 cup grated Parmesan cheese
- 1 teaspoon garlic powder
- 1/2 teaspoon salt
- 1/4 teaspoon black pepper
- 1 egg, beaten

Directions:

1. In a shallow dish, combine almond flour, grated Parmesan cheese, garlic powder, salt, and black pepper.
2. Dip each zucchini round into the beaten egg, then dredge in the almond flour mixture until well coated.
3. Preheat the air fryer to 400°F.
4. Arrange the zucchini rounds in a single layer in the air fryer basket, making sure they do not overlap.
5. Cook for 10 minutes, flipping halfway through or until the zucchini bites are golden and crispy.
6. Serve immediately.

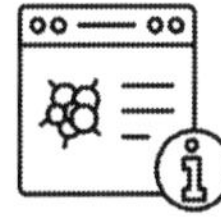

Nutritional Information: *120 calories, 6g protein, 5g carbohydrates, 8g fat, 2g fiber, 30mg cholesterol, 330mg sodium, 250mg potassium.*

6.15 Fiery Almond Snack

Yield:
4 servings

Prep time:
10 minutes

Cook time:
15 minutes

Ingredients:

- 2 cups raw almonds
- 1 tablespoon olive oil
- 1 teaspoon chili powder
- 1/2 teaspoon garlic powder
- 1/2 teaspoon onion powder
- 1/4 teaspoon cayenne pepper (adjust to taste)
- 1/2 teaspoon salt

Directions:

1. In a large bowl, mix the almonds with olive oil until they are evenly coated.
2. Add chili powder, garlic powder, onion powder, cayenne pepper, and salt to the bowl. Stir until the almonds are evenly coated with the spices.
3. Preheat the air fryer to 350°F. Once preheated, spread the almonds in an even layer in the air fryer basket. If necessary, cook in batches to avoid overcrowding.
4. Air fry the almonds for about 15 minutes, shaking the basket halfway through the cooking time to ensure even cooking.

Nutritional Information: *220 calories, 8g protein, 9g carbohydrates, 19g fat, 4g fiber, 0mg cholesterol, 300mg sodium, 250mg potassium.*

6.16 Apple Chips

Yield:
4 servings

Prep time:
10 minutes

Cook time:
20 minutes

Ingredients:

- 2 medium apples
- 1 teaspoon ground cinnamon
- 1 tablespoon erythritol (or another keto-friendly sweetener)

Directions:

1. Preheat the air fryer to 350°F.
2. Core the apples and slice them thinly using a mandoline or a sharp knife.
3. In a bowl, mix the apple slices with cinnamon and erythritol until evenly coated.
4. Place the apple slices in a single layer in the air fryer basket. Cook for 15-20 minutes, shaking the basket halfway through, until the chips are crispy.

Nutritional Information: *50 calories, 0g protein, 12g carbohydrates, 0g fat, 2g fiber, 0mg cholesterol, 0mg sodium, 100mg potassium.*

Chapter 7:

Poultry Main Dishes

Chapter 7 Fotos

7.1 Italian Herb Chicken Parmesan

Yield:
4 servings

Prep time:
15 minutes

Cook time:
12 minutes

Ingredients:

- 4 boneless, skinless chicken breasts
- 1 cup almond flour
- 1 tablespoon Italian seasoning
- 1 teaspoon garlic powder
- 1/2 teaspoon salt
- 1/4 teaspoon black pepper
- 2 large eggs
- 1/2 cup grated Parmesan cheese
- 1 cup shredded mozzarella cheese
- 1 cup low-carb marinara sauce

Directions:

1. In a shallow bowl, mix almond flour, Italian seasoning, garlic powder, salt, and black pepper. In another shallow bowl, whisk the eggs. Dip each chicken breast into the eggs, then dredge in the almond flour mixture, ensuring both sides are well coated.
2. Preheat the air fryer to 375°F. Place the coated chicken breasts in the basket, not touching each other. Cook for 6 minutes, then flip the chicken breasts over.
3. Top each chicken breast with marinara sauce, then sprinkle with Parmesan and mozzarella cheeses. Continue cooking for another 6 minutes or until the chicken is cooked through and the cheese is melted and slightly browned.
4. Let the chicken rest for a few minutes before serving.

Nutritional Information: *560 calories, 54g protein, 9g carbohydrates, 34g fat, 4g fiber, 155mg cholesterol, 690mg sodium, 450mg potassium.*

7.2 Turkey Delight Meatballs

Yield:
4 servings

Prep time:
15 minutes

Cook time:
10 minutes

Ingredients:

- 1 pound ground turkey
- 1/4 cup almond flour
- 1/4 cup grated Parmesan cheese
- 1 large egg
- 2 tablespoons fresh parsley, finely chopped
- 1 teaspoon garlic powder
- 1/2 teaspoon onion powder
- 1/2 teaspoon salt
- 1/4 teaspoon black pepper
- Cooking spray (olive oil)

Directions:

1. In a large bowl, combine ground turkey, almond flour, Parmesan cheese, egg, parsley, garlic powder, onion powder, salt, and black pepper. Mix well until all ingredients are evenly distributed.
2. Form the mixture into meatballs about 1 inch in diameter. You should get around 16 meatballs.
3. Preheat the air fryer to 400°F. Place the meatballs in the basket, making sure they are not touching to ensure even cooking.
4. Cook for 10 minutes, turning the meatballs halfway through the cooking time, until they are golden brown on the outside and cooked through.
5. Serve immediately with your favorite low-carb sauce, or enjoy them plain.

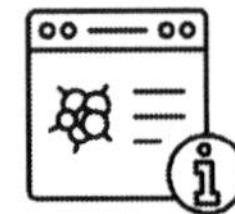

Nutritional Information: *240 calories, 28g protein, 3g carbohydrates, 14g fat, 1g fiber, 115mg cholesterol, 390mg sodium, 300mg potassium.*

7.3 Buffalo Blaze Wings

Yield:
4 servings

Prep time:
10 minutes

Cook time:
25 minutes

Ingredients:

- 2 pounds chicken wings, tips removed and wings cut into drumettes and flats
- 1 tablespoon baking powder (aluminum-free)
- 1 teaspoon garlic powder
- 1 teaspoon paprika
- 1/2 teaspoon salt
- 1/2 teaspoon black pepper
- 1/2 cup buffalo sauce (keto-friendly)
- 2 tablespoons unsalted butter, melted

Directions:

1. In a large bowl, combine baking powder, garlic powder, paprika, salt, and pepper. Add the chicken wings and toss until they are evenly coated with the seasoning mix.
2. Preheat your air fryer to 400°F. Arrange the wings in a single layer in the air fryer basket, ensuring they are not touching. You may need to cook them in batches, depending on the size of your air fryer.
3. Cook the wings for 25 minutes, flipping them halfway through the cooking time until they are golden brown and crispy.
4. While the wings are cooking, mix the buffalo sauce and melted butter in a bowl. Once the wings are done, toss them in the sauce mixture until well coated.

Nutritional Information: *535 calories, 43g protein, 0g carbohydrates, 39g fat, 0g fiber, 195mg cholesterol, 1720mg sodium, 365mg potassium.*

7.4 Tropical Chicken Skewers

Yield:
4 servings

Prep time:
20 minutes

Cook time:
10 minutes

Ingredients:

- 1.5 pounds chicken breast, cut into strips
- 1/4 cup coconut milk
- 2 tablespoons peanut butter, sugar-free
- 1 tablespoon soy sauce, low sodium
- 1 tablespoon curry powder
- 1 clove garlic, minced
- 1 teaspoon ginger, grated
- Salt and pepper to taste
- Fresh cilantro for garnish (optional)
- Lime wedges for serving (optional)

Directions:

1. In a mixing bowl, whisk together the coconut milk, peanut butter, soy sauce, curry powder, garlic, ginger, salt, and pepper until well combined. Add the chicken strips to the marinade, ensuring they are fully coated. Cover and refrigerate for at least 15 minutes or up to 4 hours for deeper flavor.
2. Preheat the air fryer to 400°F. Thread the marinated chicken strips onto skewers if using.
3. Place the chicken skewers in the air fryer basket, making sure they do not touch for even cooking. Cook for 10 minutes, turning halfway through or until the chicken is fully cooked and slightly golden.
4. Serve the chicken satay hot, garnished with fresh cilantro and lime wedges on the side, if desired.

Nutritional Information: *270 calories, 38g protein, 4g carbohydrates, 11g fat, 1g fiber, 96mg cholesterol, 330mg sodium, 650mg potassium.*

7.5 Chicken Cordon Bleu

Yield:
4 servings

Prep time:
15 minutes

Cook time:
20 minutes

Ingredients:

- 4 boneless, skinless chicken breasts
- 4 slices of ham, sugar-free
- 4 slices of Swiss cheese
- 1 cup almond flour
- 1 teaspoon garlic powder
- 1 teaspoon onion powder
- 1/2 teaspoon paprika
- Salt and pepper to taste
- 2 large eggs, beaten

Directions:

1. In a large bowl, combine baking powder, garlic powder, pal. Start by pounding the chicken breasts to about 1/4 inch thickness between two pieces of parchment paper. Season both sides with salt and pepper.
2. Place a slice of ham and a slice of Swiss cheese on each chicken breast. Roll the chicken tightly and secure it with toothpicks.
3. In a shallow dish, mix almond flour, garlic powder, onion powder, paprika, salt, and pepper. In another dish, have the beaten eggs ready.
4. Dip each chicken roll first in the beaten eggs, then in the almond flour mixture, making sure it's well coated.
5. Preheat the air fryer to 375°F. Place the chicken rolls in the basket, seam side down, and spray the tops with olive oil spray.
6. Cook for 20 minutes or until the chicken is cooked through and the coating is golden brown. Let rest for a few minutes before serving. Remove toothpicks before serving.

Nutritional Information: *355 calories, 53g protein, 5g carbohydrates, 14g fat, 2g fiber, 165mg cholesterol, 870mg sodium, 400mg potassium.*

7.6 Asian-Inspired Teriyaki Chicken Delight

Yield:
4 servings

Prep time:
10 minutes

Cook time:
20 minutes

Ingredients:

- 4 boneless, skinless chicken thighs (about 1.5 pounds)
- 1/4 cup soy sauce
- 2 tablespoons sugar-free sweetener (erythritol or monk fruit)
- 1 tablespoon apple cider vinegar
- 1 teaspoon garlic powder
- 1 teaspoon ginger powder
- 1/2 teaspoon onion powder
- Sesame seeds for garnish (optional)
- Green onions, chopped for garnish (optional)

Directions:

1. In a bowl, whisk together soy sauce, sugar-free sweetener, apple cider vinegar, garlic powder, ginger powder, and onion powder to make the teriyaki sauce.
2. Place chicken thighs in a large bowl or resealable plastic bag. Pour the teriyaki sauce over the chicken, ensuring each piece is well coated. Marinate for at least 30 minutes or overnight in the refrigerator for enhanced flavor.
3. Preheat the air fryer to 380°F. Place the chicken thighs in the air fryer basket in a single layer, ensuring they do not overlap for even cooking.
4. Cook for 10 minutes, then flip the chicken thighs over and cook for an additional 10 minutes or until the internal temperature reaches 165°F.
5. Garnish with sesame seeds and chopped green onions before serving, if desired.

Nutritional Information: *300 calories, 35g protein, 3g carbohydrates, 17g fat, 0g fiber, 145mg cholesterol, 690mg sodium, 400mg potassium.*

7.7 Duck Breast Delight

Yield:
2 servings

Prep time:
5 minutes

Cook time:
18 minutes

Ingredients:

- 2 duck breasts (about 6 ounces each)
- Salt and pepper, to taste
- 1 teaspoon garlic powder
- 1 teaspoon dried thyme
- 1 tablespoon olive oil (for brushing)

Directions:

1. Score the skin of the duck breasts in a crosshatch pattern, being careful not to cut into the meat. Season both sides of the duck breasts with salt, pepper, garlic powder, and dried thyme.
2. Preheat the air fryer to 360°F. Brush the duck breasts lightly with olive oil.
3. Place the duck breasts, skin side down, in the air fryer basket. Cook for 10 minutes.
4. Flip the duck breasts over and cook for an additional 8 minutes or until the internal temperature reaches 135°F for medium-rare.
5. Let the duck rest for 5 minutes before slicing. This will help retain the juices and ensure the duck is moist and flavorful.

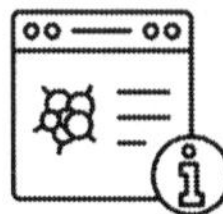

Nutritional Information: *280 calories, 34g protein, 0g carbohydrates, 16g fat, 0g fiber, 195mg cholesterol, 125mg sodium, 350mg potassium.*

7.8 Tex-Mex Chicken Strips

Yield:
4 servings

Prep time:
15 minutes

Cook time:
20 minutes

Ingredients:

- 1.5 pounds chicken breast, thinly sliced
- 1 red bell pepper, thinly sliced
- 1 green bell pepper, thinly sliced
- 1 yellow bell pepper, thinly sliced
- 1 onion, thinly sliced
- 2 tablespoons olive oil
- 1 teaspoon chili powder
- 1 teaspoon cumin
- 1/2 teaspoon garlic powder
- 1/2 teaspoon onion powder
- 1/2 teaspoon paprika
- Salt and pepper, to taste

Directions:

1. In a large bowl, combine the chicken, bell peppers, onion, olive oil, chili powder, cumin, garlic powder, onion powder, paprika, salt, and pepper. Toss everything together until the chicken and vegetables are well coated with the seasoning.
2. Preheat the air fryer to 400°F. Place the chicken and vegetable mixture in the air fryer basket. Try to spread them out into a single layer as much as possible for even cooking.
3. Cook for 10 minutes, then shake the basket or use tongs to stir the mixture to ensure even cooking. Continue cooking for another 10 minutes or until the chicken is cooked through and the vegetables are tender and slightly charred.
4. Serve immediately. For a keto-friendly serving option, enjoy your fajitas over a bed of lettuce, wrapped in a low-carb tortilla, or with a side of guacamole and sour cream.

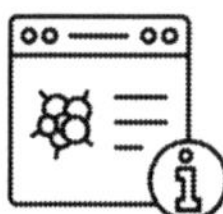

Nutritional Information: *280 calories, 34g protein, 8g carbohydrates, 12g fat, 2g fiber, 85mg cholesterol, 220mg sodium, 600mg potassium.*

7.9 Lemon & Herb Chicken Bliss

 Yield: **4 servings**

Prep time: **10 minutes**

 Cook time: **20 minutes**

Ingredients:

- 4 boneless, skinless chicken breasts
- 2 tablespoons olive oil
- 1 lemon, juiced and zested
- 2 cloves garlic, minced
- 1 teaspoon dried oregano
- 1 teaspoon dried basil
- 1 teaspoon dried thyme
- Salt and pepper to taste

Directions:

1. In a small bowl, mix together the olive oil, lemon juice, zest, minced garlic oregano, basil, thyme, salt, and pepper.
2. Place the chicken breasts in a shallow dish or a resealable plastic bag. Pour the marinade over the chicken, making sure each piece is well coated. Let marinate in the refrigerator for at least 30 minutes or up to 4 hours for more flavor.
3. Preheat the air fryer to 360°F. Place the marinated chicken breasts in the air fryer basket, ensuring they are not touching for even cooking.
4. Cook for 10 minutes, then flip the chicken breasts over and cook for another 10 minutes or until the chicken reaches an internal temperature of 165°F. Cooking times may vary based on the thickness of the chicken breasts.

Nutritional Information: *245 calories, 26g protein, 3g carbohydrates, 14g fat, 1g fiber, 65mg cholesterol, 200mg sodium, 300mg potassium.*

7.10 Cheesy Chicken Alfredo Spirals

 Yield: **4 servings**

 Prep time: **20 minutes**

 Cook time: **25 minutes**

Ingredients:

- 4 large chicken breasts, pounded to 1/4 inch thickness
- 1 cup of homemade or store-bought low-carb Alfredo sauce
- 1 cup of shredded mozzarella cheese
- 1/2 cup of grated Parmesan cheese
- 1 teaspoon of garlic powder
- 1 teaspoon of Italian seasoning
- Salt and pepper to taste
- 1 tablespoon of olive oil
- 2 cups of fresh spinach, roughly chopped

Directions:

1. Preheat your air fryer to 375°F. In a small bowl, mix the Alfredo sauce with garlic powder, Italian seasoning, salt, and pepper. In another bowl, mix the mozzarella cheese with Parmesan cheese.
2. Lay out the chicken breasts on a clean surface. Spread a spoonful of the Alfredo sauce mixture over each chicken breast, then top with chopped spinach and a sprinkle of the cheese mixture. Roll up the chicken breasts tightly and secure them with toothpicks.
3. Brush the outside of each chicken roll-up with olive oil. Place the chicken roll-ups in the basket, making sure they do not touch.
4. Cook in the air fryer for 25 minutes or until the chicken is fully cooked (internal temperature reaches 165°F). Halfway through cooking, flip the chicken roll-ups to ensure even cooking.
5. Let the chicken rest for a few minutes before removing the toothpicks, slicing, and serving with additional Alfredo sauce if desired.

Nutritional Information: *495 calories, 58g protein, 5g carbohydrates, 27g fat, 1g fiber, 165mg cholesterol, 690mg sodium, 500mg potassium.*

7.11 Creamy Chicken and Broccoli Bake

Yield:
4 servings

Prep time:
15 minutes

Cook time:
20 minutes

Ingredients:

- 2 cups of cooked chicken, shredded
- 3 cups of broccoli florets, steamed until just tender
- 1 cup of heavy cream
- 1/2 cup of chicken broth
- 2 cups of shredded cheddar cheese
- 1 teaspoon of garlic powder
- 1 teaspoon of onion powder
- Salt and pepper to taste
- 1/4 cup of grated Parmesan cheese for topping
- 2 tablespoons of almond flour for topping

Directions:

1. In a large bowl, combine the shredded chicken, steamed broccoli, heavy cream, chicken broth, shredded cheddar cheese, garlic powder, onion powder, salt, and pepper. Mix well to ensure the ingredients are evenly distributed.
2. Transfer the mixture to an air fryer-safe casserole dish or pan. In a small bowl, mix the grated Parmesan cheese with almond flour and sprinkle this topping evenly over the casserole.
3. Place the casserole dish in the air fryer basket. Set the air fryer to 375°F and cook for 20 minutes or until the casserole is bubbly and the topping has turned golden brown.
4. Let the casserole cool for a few minutes before serving. This allows the flavors to meld together and the casserole to set, making it easier to serve.

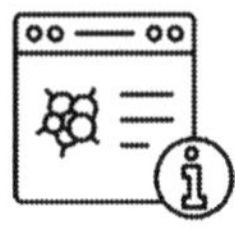
Nutritional Information: *580 calories, 45g protein, 8g carbohydrates, 42g fat, 2g fiber, 220mg cholesterol, 760mg sodium, 400mg potassium.*

7.12 Aegean Delight Chicken Skewers

Yield:
4 servings

Prep time:
15 minutes

Cook time:
10 minutes

Ingredients:

- 1 1/2 pounds of chicken breast, cut into 1-inch cubes
- 1/4 cup of olive oil
- 2 tablespoons of lemon juice
- 1 tablespoon of red wine vinegar
- 2 cloves of garlic, minced
- 1 teaspoon of dried oregano
- 1/2 teaspoon of dried thyme
- Salt and pepper to taste
- 1 bell pepper, cut into 1-inch pieces (optional for added color and nutrients)
- 1 red onion, cut into 1-inch pieces (optional)
- Wooden or metal skewers (if using wooden, soak in water for at least 30 minutes before grilling)

Directions:

1. In a large bowl, whisk together olive oil, lemon juice, red wine vinegar, minced garlic, dried oregano, dried thyme, salt, and pepper. Add the chicken cubes to the marinade, ensuring they are well coated. Cover and refrigerate for at least 1 hour or overnight for the best flavor.
2. If using wooden skewers, remember to soak them in water. Preheat the air fryer to 400°F. Thread the marinated chicken pieces onto skewers, alternating with pieces of bell pepper and red onion if using.
3. Place the skewers in the air fryer basket, ensuring they don't touch each other. Cook for 10 minutes, turning halfway through or until the chicken is fully cooked and has reached an internal temperature of 165°F.
4. Serve immediately, garnished with fresh lemon wedges and a sprinkle of fresh chopped herbs, such as parsley or dill, if desired.

Nutritional Information: *310 calories, 35g protein, 4g carbohydrates, 17g fat, 1g fiber, 165mg cholesterol, 300mg sodium, 600mg potassium.*

7.13 Spiced Chicken Tikka Bites

Yield:
4 servings

Prep time:
15 minutes

Cook time:
15 minutes

Ingredients:

- 1 1/2 pounds of chicken breast, cut into 1-inch pieces
- 1/2 cup of full-fat Greek yogurt
- 2 tablespoons of lemon juice
- 1 tablespoon of olive oil
- 2 cloves of garlic, minced
- 1 tablespoon of grated ginger
- 1 teaspoon of turmeric powder
- 1 teaspoon of cumin powder
- 1 teaspoon of coriander powder
- 1/2 teaspoon of smoked paprika
- 1/2 teaspoon of garam masala
- Salt and pepper to taste
- Fresh cilantro for garnish (optional)

Directions:

1. In a large bowl, combine the Greek yogurt, lemon juice, olive oil, minced garlic, grated ginger, turmeric, cumin, coriander, smoked paprika, garam masala, salt, and pepper. Mix well to create a marinade.
2. Add the chicken pieces to the marinade, ensuring they are well coated. Cover and refrigerate for at least 2 hours or overnight for the best flavor.
3. Preheat the air fryer to 400°F. Place the marinated chicken pieces in the air fryer basket, making sure they do not touch each other for even cooking.
4. Cook for 15 minutes, turning the pieces halfway through the cooking time or until the chicken is fully cooked and has a slight char on the outside.
5. Garnish with fresh cilantro before serving, if desired.

Nutritional Information: *265 calories, 38g protein, 3g carbohydrates, 11g fat, 1g fiber, 105mg cholesterol, 200mg sodium, 600mg potassium.*

7.14 Southwest Spice Chicken Thighs

Yield:
4 servings

Prep time:
10 minutes

Cook time:
20 minutes

Ingredients:

- 4 boneless, skinless chicken thighs
- 2 tablespoons olive oil
- 1 teaspoon garlic powder
- 1 teaspoon onion powder
- 1 teaspoon smoked paprika
- 1/2 teaspoon ground cumin
- 1/2 teaspoon chili powder
- Salt and pepper to taste
- 1/4 cup fresh cilantro, chopped (for garnish)
- Lime wedges for serving

Directions:

1. Preheat the air fryer to 380°F. In a small bowl, combine the olive oil, garlic powder, onion powder, smoked paprika, ground cumin, chili powder, salt, and pepper. Mix well to create a marinade.
2. Coat the chicken thighs evenly with the marinade. Let them sit for about 5 minutes to absorb the flavors.
3. Place the chicken thighs in the air fryer basket in a single layer, ensuring they do not touch each other for even cooking.
4. Cook for 20 minutes, turning the thighs halfway through the cooking time or until the chicken is fully cooked and the internal temperature reaches 165°F.
5. Serve the chicken thighs garnished with fresh cilantro and lime wedges on the side.

Nutritional Information: *310 calories, 24g protein, 2g carbohydrates, 23g fat, 0g fiber, 142mg cholesterol, 620mg sodium, 300mg potassium.*

7.15 Keto Chicken Schnitzel

Yield:
4 servings

Prep time:
15 minutes

Cook time:
12 minutes

Ingredients:

- 4 boneless, skinless chicken breasts, pounded to 1/4 inch thickness
- 1 cup almond flour
- 2 large eggs, beaten
- 1 teaspoon garlic powder
- 1 teaspoon paprika
- Salt and pepper to taste
- 2 tablespoons grated Parmesan cheese (optional)

Directions:

1. In one shallow bowl, mix the almond flour with garlic powder, paprika, salt, pepper, and grated Parmesan cheese (if using). Place the beaten eggs in another shallow bowl.
2. Dredge each chicken breast first in the egg mixture, allowing the excess to drip off, then coat evenly with the almond flour mixture. Make sure the chicken is fully coated.
3. Preheat the air fryer to 400°F.
4. Place the coated chicken breasts in the air fryer basket in a single layer, making sure they do not touch. You may need to cook in batches depending on the size of your air fryer.
5. Cook for 6 minutes, then flip the chicken breasts. Continue cooking for another 6 minutes or until the chicken is golden brown and reaches an internal temperature of 165°F.
6. Serve immediately with a side of your choice or a fresh salad to keep it keto-friendly.

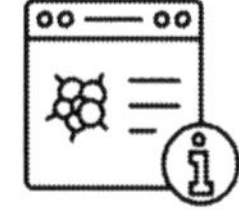

Nutritional Information: *350 calories, 32g protein, 4g carbohydrates, 22g fat, 2g fiber, 145mg cholesterol, 200mg sodium, 300mg potassium.*

Chapter 8:

Meat Main Dishes: Beef, Pork, Lamb

8.1 Golden Keto Empanadas

Yield:
4 servings

Prep time:
25 minutes

Cook time:
8 minutes

Ingredients:

For the dough:

- 1 1/2 cups almond flour
- 1/4 cup coconut flour
- 1 teaspoon xanthan gum
- 1/2 teaspoon salt
- 4 tablespoons unsalted butter, melted
- 1 large egg

For the filling:

- 1 tablespoon olive oil
- 1/2 pound ground beef
- 1/2 small onion, finely chopped
- 1 clove garlic, minced
- 1/2 teaspoon cumin
- 1/2 teaspoon smoked paprika
- Salt and pepper to taste
- 1/4 cup shredded cheddar cheese

Directions:

1. To make the dough, mix almond flour, coconut flour, xanthan gum, and salt in a bowl. Add melted butter and egg, mixing until a dough forms. If the dough is too sticky, add a bit more almond flour until it's manageable. Chill in the refrigerator for 10 minutes.
2. For the filling, heat olive oil in a skillet over medium heat. Add ground beef, onion, and garlic. Cook until the beef is browned, and the onions are translucent. Stir in cumin, smoked paprika, salt, and pepper. Remove from heat and let it cool slightly. Stir in shredded cheddar cheese.
3. Preheat the air fryer to 350°F. Divide the dough into 8 equal parts. Roll each part into a ball, then flatten it into a disc. Place a spoonful of the beef mixture in the center of each disc. Fold the dough over the filling to create a half-moon shape, pressing the edges to seal.
4. Place the empanadas in the air fryer basket, making sure they don't touch. Cook for 8 minutes or until golden brown.
5. Serve hot with your favorite keto-friendly dipping sauce.

Nutritional Information: *Approximately 400 calories, 25g protein, 10g carbohydrates, 30g fat, 5g fiber, 100mg cholesterol, 300mg sodium, 200mg potassium.*

8.2 Herb-Seasoned Pork Chops

Yield:
4 servings

Prep time:
10 minutes

Cook time:
15 minutes

Ingredients:

- 4 boneless pork chops, about 1 inch thick
- 1 tablespoon olive oil
- 1 teaspoon garlic powder
- 1 teaspoon onion powder
- 1 teaspoon smoked paprika
- 1/2 teaspoon salt
- 1/4 teaspoon black pepper
- 1/4 teaspoon dried thyme

Directions:

1. Preheat your air fryer to 380°F. In a small bowl, mix together the garlic powder, onion powder, smoked paprika, salt, black pepper, and dried thyme.
2. Brush both sides of each pork chop with olive oil, then evenly sprinkle the seasoning mix over the pork chops, pressing gently to adhere.
3. Place the pork chops in the air fryer basket, ensuring they are not touching for proper air circulation. Cook for 10-15 minutes, flipping halfway through or until the pork chops are cooked through and have reached an internal temperature of 145°F.
4. Let the pork chops rest for 3 minutes before serving to allow the juices to redistribute.

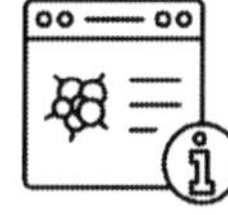

Nutritional Information: *230 calories, 29g protein, 0g carbohydrates, 13g fat, 0g fiber, 80mg cholesterol, 330mg sodium, 500mg potassium.*

8.3 Rosemary-Infused Lamb Chops

Yield:
4 servings

Prep time:
15 minutes

Cook time:
12 minutes

Ingredients:

- 8 lamb chops, about 1 inch thick
- 2 tablespoons olive oil
- 2 tablespoons fresh rosemary, chopped
- 2 cloves garlic, minced
- 1/2 teaspoon salt
- 1/4 teaspoon black pepper

Directions:

1. In a small bowl, combine the olive oil, chopped rosemary, minced garlic, salt, and black pepper. Mix well.
2. Rub the mixture evenly over both sides of the lamb chops. Let them marinate for at least 10 minutes to absorb the flavors.
3. Preheat the air fryer to 400°F. Arrange the lamb chops in the air fryer basket in a single layer, ensuring they are not touching for optimal air circulation.
4. Cook for 6 minutes, then flip the lamb chops over and cook for an additional 6 minutes or until they reach your desired level of doneness.
5. Let the lamb chops rest for a few minutes before serving to allow the juices to redistribute.

Nutritional Information: *310 calories, 19g protein, 0g carbohydrates, 26g fat, 0g fiber, 85mg cholesterol, 370mg sodium, 290mg potassium.*

8.4 Savory Beef Stick Delights

Yield:
4 servings

Prep time:
20 minutes

Cook time:
10 minutes

Ingredients:

- 1 lb beef sirloin, cut into 1-inch cubes
- 2 tablespoons olive oil
- 1 teaspoon garlic powder
- 1 teaspoon onion powder
- 1/2 teaspoon smoked paprika
- 1/2 teaspoon salt
- 1/4 teaspoon black pepper
- Wooden skewers, soaked in water for 30 minutes

Directions:

1. In a large bowl, combine the olive oil, garlic powder, onion powder, smoked paprika, salt, and black pepper. Add the beef cubes to the bowl and toss to coat evenly with the seasoning mix. Let marinate for at least 15 minutes to enhance the flavors.
2. Preheat the air fryer to 400°F. Thread the marinated beef cubes onto the soaked skewers, leaving a small space between each piece to ensure even cooking.
3. Place the skewers in the air fryer basket, making sure they do not touch each other. Cook for 10 minutes, turning the skewers halfway through the cooking time or until the beef is cooked to your desired level of doneness.
4. Remove the skewers from the air fryer and let rest for a few minutes before serving.

Nutritional Information: *280 calories, 26g protein, 0g carbohydrates, 19g fat, 0g fiber, 65mg cholesterol, 330mg sodium, 400mg potassium.*

8.5 Tender Pork Belly Cubes

Yield:
4 servings

Prep time:
10 minutes

Cook time:
20 minutes

Ingredients:

- 1 lb pork belly, cut into 1-inch cubes
- 1 tablespoon olive oil
- 1 teaspoon salt
- 1/2 teaspoon black pepper
- 1/2 teaspoon garlic powder
- 1/2 teaspoon onion powder
- 1/4 teaspoon smoked paprika

Directions:

1. Preheat the air fryer to 400°F. In a large bowl, mix together the olive oil, salt, black pepper, garlic powder, onion powder, and smoked paprika.
2. Add the pork belly cubes to the bowl and toss until they are evenly coated with the seasoning mix.
3. Place the pork belly cubes in the air fryer basket, ensuring they are spaced apart for even cooking. Cook for 20 minutes, shaking the basket halfway through the cooking time to ensure even browning.
4. Once cooked, let the pork belly bites rest for a few minutes before serving. They should be crispy on the outside and tender on the inside.

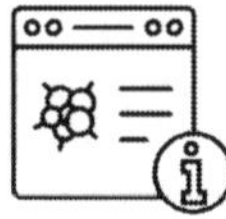

Nutritional Information: *620 calories, 14g protein, 0g carbohydrates, 62g fat, 0g fiber, 180mg cholesterol, 620mg sodium, 0mg potassium.*

8.6 Flavorful Beef Loaf

Yield:
4 servings

Prep time:
15 minutes

Cook time:
25 minutes

Ingredients:

- 1 lb ground beef (80/20 mix)
- 1/2 cup almond flour
- 1 large egg
- 1/4 cup grated Parmesan cheese
- 2 tablespoons tomato paste
- 1 tablespoon Worcestershire sauce
- 1 teaspoon garlic powder
- 1 teaspoon onion powder
- 1/2 teaspoon salt
- 1/4 teaspoon black pepper
- 1/4 cup fresh parsley, finely chopped

Directions:

1. In a large bowl, combine ground beef, almond flour, egg, Parmesan cheese, tomato paste, Worcestershire sauce, garlic powder, onion powder, salt, black pepper, and parsley. Mix well until all ingredients are evenly distributed.
2. Form the mixture into a loaf shape that will fit in your air fryer basket. If your air fryer has a rack, you can place the meatloaf on parchment paper for easier removal after cooking.
3. Preheat the air fryer to 360°F. Place the meatloaf in the air fryer basket and cook for 25 minutes or until the internal temperature reaches 160°F. If the meatloaf starts to brown too much on top, you can cover it with a piece of aluminum foil.
4. Once cooked, let the meatloaf rest for a few minutes before slicing and serving.

Nutritional Information: *498 calories, 31g protein, 4g carbohydrates, 38g fat, 2g fiber, 145mg cholesterol, 634mg sodium, 349mg potassium.*

8.7 Beef & Cauliflower Rice Stuffed Peppers

Yield:
4 servings

Prep time:
20 minutes

Cook time:
15 minutes

Ingredients:

- 4 medium bell peppers, tops removed and seeded
- 1 lb ground beef (85/15 mix)
- 1/2 cup cauliflower rice, cooked
- 1/4 cup onion, finely chopped
- 1 clove garlic, minced
- 1 teaspoon cumin
- 1 teaspoon chili powder
- 1/2 teaspoon salt
- 1/4 teaspoon black pepper
- 1/2 cup shredded cheddar cheese
- 1/4 cup fresh cilantro, chopped (optional for garnish)

Directions:

1. In a skillet over medium heat, cook the ground beef, onion, and garlic until the beef is browned. Drain any excess fat.
2. Stir in the cumin, chili powder, salt, and black pepper. Add the cooked cauliflower rice to the beef mixture and mix well.
3. Preheat the air fryer to 350°F. Spoon the beef and cauliflower rice mixture into the hollowed-out bell peppers.
4. Place the stuffed peppers in the air fryer basket. Cook for 15 minutes or until the peppers are tender.
5. In the last 2 minutes of cooking, sprinkle the shredded cheddar cheese over the top of each pepper. Continue cooking until the cheese is melted and bubbly.
6. Garnish with chopped cilantro before serving, if desired.

Nutritional Information: *320 calories, 23g protein, 12g carbohydrates, 20g fat, 3g fiber, 80mg cholesterol, 600mg sodium, 650mg potassium.*

8.8 Classic Ribeye

Yield:
2 servings

Prep time:
5 minutes

Cook time:
12 minutes

Ingredients:

- 2 ribeye steaks, about 1 inch thick
- 1 tablespoon olive oil
- 1 teaspoon salt
- 1/2 teaspoon black pepper
- 1/2 teaspoon garlic powder
- 1/2 teaspoon onion powder

Directions:

1. Preheat the air fryer to 400°F. Brush both sides of the ribeye steaks with olive oil.
2. Combine salt, black pepper, garlic powder, and onion powder in a small bowl. Sprinkle the seasoning mix evenly over both sides of the steaks, pressing gently to adhere.
3. Place the steaks in the air fryer basket, making sure they are not touching for optimal air circulation.
4. Cook for about 12 minutes for medium-rare, flipping halfway through the cooking time. Adjust the cooking time according to your preferred level of doneness.
5. Let the steaks rest for a few minutes before serving to allow the juices to redistribute.

Nutritional Information: *470 calories, 46g protein, 0g carbohydrates, 32g fat, 0g fiber, 137mg cholesterol, 590mg sodium, 608mg potassium.*

8.9 Bacon-Encased Pork Delicacy

Yield:
4 servings

Prep time:
10 minutes

Cook time:
20 minutes

Ingredients:

- 1 pork tenderloin (about 1 lb)
- 8-10 slices of bacon
- 1 teaspoon salt
- 1/2 teaspoon black pepper
- 1 teaspoon garlic powder
- 1/2 teaspoon onion powder
- 1/2 teaspoon smoked paprika

Directions:

1. Preheat the air fryer to 400°F. In a small bowl, mix together salt, black pepper, garlic powder, onion powder, and smoked paprika.
2. Rub the spice mix all over the pork tenderloin. Wrap the tenderloin evenly with the bacon slices, making sure to overlap them slightly to cover the pork completely.
3. Place the bacon-wrapped pork tenderloin in the air fryer basket. Cook for 20 minutes or until the bacon is crispy and the pork reaches an internal temperature of 145°F. Halfway through the cooking time, flip the tenderloin to ensure even cooking.
4. Let the pork tenderloin rest for a few minutes before slicing and serving.

Nutritional Information: *310 calories, 35g protein, 0g carbohydrates, 18g fat, 0g fiber, 105mg cholesterol, 870mg sodium, 590mg potassium.*

8.10 Mint Lamb Meatballs

Yield:
4 servings

Prep time:
15 minutes

Cook time:
10 minutes

Ingredients:

- 1 lb ground lamb
- 1/4 cup almond flour
- 1 large egg
- 2 cloves garlic, minced
- 2 tablespoons fresh mint, finely chopped
- 1 tablespoon fresh parsley, finely chopped
- 1 teaspoon cumin
- 1/2 teaspoon salt
- 1/4 teaspoon black pepper

Directions:

1. In a large bowl, combine the ground lamb, almond flour, egg, minced garlic, chopped mint, chopped parsley, cumin, salt, and black pepper. Mix well until all the ingredients are evenly distributed.
2. Form the mixture into meatballs about 1 inch in diameter.
3. Place the meatballs in the basket, making sure they are not touching to ensure even cooking.
4. Preheat the air fryer to 400°F. Cook the meatballs for 10 minutes or until they are browned on the outside and reach an internal temperature of 160°F.
5. Serve the meatballs hot, with your choice of low-carb sides or dipping sauces.

Nutritional Information: *330 calories, 20g protein, 3g carbohydrates, 26g fat, 1g fiber, 105mg cholesterol, 370mg sodium, 290mg potassium.*

8.11 Pork Carnitas with Lime

Yield:
4 servings

Prep time:
10 minutes

Cook time:
25 minutes

Ingredients:

- 2 lbs pork shoulder, cut into 2-inch cubes
- 1 tablespoon olive oil
- 1 teaspoon salt
- 1/2 teaspoon black pepper
- 1 teaspoon garlic powder
- 1 teaspoon cumin
- 1/2 teaspoon oregano
- 1/4 teaspoon chili powder
- Juice of 1 lime
- 1/4 cup chicken broth

Directions:

1. In a large bowl, combine olive oil, salt, black pepper, garlic powder, cumin, oregano, chili powder, and lime juice. Add the pork shoulder cubes and toss to coat evenly with the seasoning.
2. Place the pork cubes in the air fryer basket. Pour the chicken broth over the pork. This will help to keep the meat moist during cooking.
3. Preheat the air fryer to 400°F. Cook the pork for 25 minutes, shaking the basket halfway through to ensure even cooking. The pork should be tender and easily shreddable.
4. Remove the pork from the air fryer and let it cool slightly before shredding it with two forks. The carnitas can be served in a variety of ways, such as in keto tacos, over salads, or as a main dish with low-carb sides.

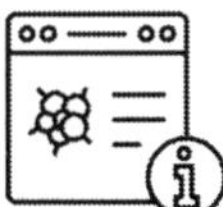

Nutritional Information: *310 calories, 32g protein, 0g carbohydrates, 20g fat, 0g fiber, 95mg cholesterol, 630mg sodium, 500mg potassium.*

8.12 Mushroom-Infused Stroganoff Balls

Yield:
4 servings

Prep time:
15 minutes

Cook time:
15 minutes

Ingredients:

For the meatballs:

- 1 lb ground beef
- 1/4 cup almond flour
- 1 large egg
- 1/2 teaspoon salt
- 1/4 teaspoon black pepper
- 1 teaspoon garlic powder
- 1/2 teaspoon onion powder

For the sauce:

- 1 cup heavy cream
- 1/2 cup beef broth
- 2 tablespoons Worcestershire sauce
- 1 teaspoon Dijon mustard
- Salt and pepper to taste
- 1 tablespoon olive oil
- 1/2 onion, finely chopped
- 1 clove garlic, minced
- 8 oz mushrooms, sliced

Directions:

1. In a large bowl, mix together ground beef, almond flour, egg, salt, black pepper, garlic powder, and onion powder. Form into meatballs, about 1 inch in diameter.
2. Preheat the air fryer to 400°F. Place the meatballs in the air fryer basket, ensuring they are not touching. Cook for 15 minutes or until they are browned and cooked through.
3. While the meatballs are cooking, prepare the sauce. In a large skillet over medium heat, add olive oil, onion, and garlic. Sauté until the onion is translucent and the garlic is fragrant.
4. Add mushrooms to the skillet and cook until they are soft. Stir in heavy cream, beef broth, Worcestershire sauce, and Dijon mustard. Bring to a simmer and cook until the sauce thickens slightly. Season with salt and pepper to taste.
5. Once meatballs are done, add them to the skillet with the sauce. Stir to coat the meatballs in the sauce.
6. Serve the beef stroganoff meatballs hot, garnished with fresh parsley if desired.

Nutritional Information: *520 calories, 28g protein, 8g carbohydrates, 42g fat, 2g fiber, 175mg cholesterol, 690mg sodium, 400mg potassium.*

8.13 Rustic Sausage-Cabbage Medley

 Yield: **4 servings**

 Prep time: **10 minutes**

Cook time: **15 minutes**

Ingredients:

- 1 lb smoked sausage, sliced into 1/2-inch pieces
- 1 small head of cabbage, cored and chopped into bite-sized pieces
- 1 tablespoon olive oil
- 1 teaspoon salt
- 1/2 teaspoon black pepper
- 1/2 teaspoon garlic powder
- 1/2 teaspoon onion powder

Directions:

1. In a large bowl, toss the chopped cabbage with olive oil, salt, black pepper, garlic powder, and onion powder until the cabbage is evenly coated.
2. Add the sliced sausage to the bowl with the cabbage and toss to combine.
3. Preheat the air fryer to 400°F. Transfer the sausage and cabbage mixture to the air fryer basket, spreading it out evenly.
4. Cook for 15 minutes, stirring halfway through the cooking time, until the cabbage is tender and the sausage is browned.
5. Serve hot as a delicious low-carb meal.

Nutritional Information: *320 calories, 18g protein, 9g carbohydrates, 24g fat, 3g fiber, 60mg cholesterol, 870mg sodium, 400mg potassium.*

8.14 Tender Pulled Pork Perfection

 Yield: **4 servings**

 Prep time: **10 minutes**

 Cook time: **60 minutes**

Ingredients:

- 2 lbs pork shoulder, cut into 2-inch cubes
- 2 tablespoons olive oil
- 1 tablespoon smoked paprika
- 1 tablespoon garlic powder
- 1 teaspoon salt
- 1/2 teaspoon black pepper
- 1/2 cup chicken broth

Directions:

1. In a large bowl, combine the olive oil, smoked paprika, garlic powder, salt, and black pepper. Add the pork shoulder cubes and toss until they are well coated with the seasoning mix.
2. Place the seasoned pork cubes in the air fryer basket. Pour the chicken broth around the pork in the basket. This will help keep the pork moist during cooking.
3. Preheat the air fryer to 320°F. Cook the pork for 60 minutes or until it is very tender and shreds easily with a fork. You may need to cook in batches, depending on the size of your air fryer.
4. Once cooked, remove the pork from the air fryer and let it rest for a few minutes. Then, using two forks, shred the pork into pieces.
5. Serve the pulled pork hot, with your choice of keto-friendly sides, or use it as a filling for keto tacos or salads.

Nutritional Information: *470 calories, 38g protein, 0g carbohydrates, 35g fat, 0g fiber, 140mg cholesterol, 660mg sodium, 600mg potassium.*

8.15 Beef Jerky

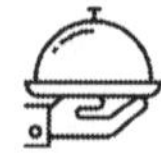
Yield:
6 servings

Prep time:
30 minutes

Cook time:
3-4 hours

Ingredients:

- 2 lbs lean beef (top round, flank steak or similar), thinly sliced
- 1/2 cup soy sauce
- 2 tablespoons Worcestershire sauce
- 1 tablespoon apple cider vinegar
- 1 tablespoon olive oil
- 2 teaspoons garlic powder
- 2 teaspoons onion powder
- 1 teaspoon black pepper
- 1/2 teaspoon red pepper flakes (optional for heat)

Directions:

1. In a large bowl, mix together soy sauce, Worcestershire sauce, apple cider vinegar, olive oil, garlic powder, onion powder, black pepper, and red pepper flakes (if using) to create the marinade.
2. Add the thinly sliced beef to the marinade, ensuring each piece is well coated. Cover and refrigerate for at least 4 hours or overnight for best results.
3. Preheat the air fryer to 180°F. Place a rack or use foil with holes poked in it in the air fryer basket to allow for airflow around the beef slices.
4. Arrange the beef slices in a single layer on the rack, making sure they are not touching. You may need to work in batches depending on the size of your air fryer.
5. Cook for 3-4 hours, flipping the beef slices halfway through the cooking time, until the beef jerky is dry and leathery but still pliable.
6. 6. Allow the beef jerky to cool before storing it in an airtight container. The jerky can be stored at room temperature for up to 2 weeks.

Nutritional Information (per serving): *Approximately 250 calories, 36g protein, 3g carbohydrates, 10g fat, 0g fiber, 70mg cholesterol, 1000mg sodium, 500mg potassium.*

Chapter 9:

Seafood and Fish Main Dishes

Chapter 9 Fotos

9.1 Lemon Dill Salmon Elegance

Yield:
4 servings

Prep time:
15 minutes

Cook time:
10 minutes

Ingredients:

- 4 salmon fillets (about 6 ounces each)
- 2 tablespoons olive oil
- 1/2 teaspoon salt
- 1/4 teaspoon black pepper
- 1 lemon, sliced

For the Dill Sauce:

- 1/2 cup sour cream
- 2 tablespoons mayonnaise
- 2 tablespoons fresh dill, chopped
- 1 tablespoon lemon juice
- 1/4 teaspoon garlic powder
- Salt and pepper to taste

Directions:

1. Preheat your air fryer to 400°F. Rub each salmon fillet with olive oil and season with salt and pepper. Place lemon slices on top of each fillet.
2. Arrange the salmon fillets in the air fryer basket, ensuring they are not touching. Cook for 10 minutes or until the salmon easily flakes with a fork.
3. While the salmon is cooking, prepare the dill sauce by mixing sour cream, mayonnaise, dill, lemon juice, and garlic powder in a small bowl. Season with salt and pepper to taste.
4. Once the salmon is cooked, serve immediately with the dill sauce on the side.

Nutritional Information: *354 calories, 34g protein, 3g carbohydrates, 23g fat, 0g fiber, 89mg cholesterol, 397mg sodium, 834mg potassium.*

9.2 Lemon Simplicity Cod

Yield:
4 servings

Prep time:
10 minutes

Cook time:
12 minutes

Ingredients:

- 4 cod fillets (about 6 ounces each)
- 1 tablespoon olive oil
- 1/2 teaspoon garlic powder
- 1/2 teaspoon paprika
- Salt and pepper to taste
- 1 lemon, cut into wedges for serving

Directions:

1. Preheat the air fryer to 400°F. In a small bowl, mix together olive oil, garlic powder, paprika, salt, and pepper.
2. Brush each cod fillet with the olive oil mixture, ensuring all sides are coated.
3. Place the cod fillets in the air fryer basket in a single layer, ensuring they are not touching.
4. Cook for 12 minutes or until the cod is opaque and flakes easily with a fork. Depending on the thickness of your fillets, cooking time may need to be adjusted.
5. Serve immediately with lemon wedges on the side.

Nutritional Information: *190 calories, 23g protein, 0g carbohydrates, 10g fat, 0g fiber, 60mg cholesterol, 70mg sodium, 520mg potassium.*

9.3 Italian Herb Tuna Elegance

Yield:
4 servings

Prep time:
10 minutes

Cook time:
8 minutes

Ingredients:

- 4 tuna steaks (about 6 ounces each)
- 2 tablespoons olive oil
- 1 teaspoon garlic powder
- 1 teaspoon dried Italian herbs
- Salt and pepper to taste
- Lemon wedges for serving

Directions:

1. Preheat your air fryer to 400°F. In a small bowl, mix together the olive oil, garlic powder, Italian herbs, salt, and pepper.
2. Brush each tuna steak with the olive oil mixture, ensuring all sides are well coated.
3. Place the tuna steaks in the air fryer basket, making sure they do not touch.
4. Cook for 4 minutes, then flip the steaks and cook for an additional 4 minutes or until the tuna is cooked to your desired level of doneness.
5. Serve immediately with lemon wedges on the side.

Nutritional Information: *220 calories, 30g protein, 0g carbohydrates, 10g fat, 0g fiber, 45mg cholesterol, 65mg sodium, 500mg potassium.*

9.4 Shrimp Scampi

Yield:
4 servings

Prep time:
10 minutes

Cook time:
8 minutes

Ingredients:

- 1 pound large shrimp, peeled and deveined
- 2 tablespoons olive oil
- 3 garlic cloves, minced
- 1/2 teaspoon red pepper flakes (optional)
- Juice of 1 lemon
- 2 tablespoons fresh parsley, chopped
- Salt and pepper to taste

Directions:

1. In a bowl, combine shrimp, olive oil, garlic, red pepper flakes (if using), lemon juice, parsley, salt, and pepper. Toss to coat the shrimp evenly.
2. Preheat the air fryer to 400°F. Place the shrimp in the air fryer basket in a single layer, ensuring they are not overcrowded.
3. Cook for 4 minutes, then shake the basket or turn the shrimp over, and cook for an additional 4 minutes or until the shrimp are pink and cooked through.
4. Serve immediately, garnished with more parsley if desired.

Nutritional Information: *170 calories, 24g protein, 2g carbohydrates, 7g fat, 0g fiber, 182mg cholesterol, 300mg sodium, 220mg potassium.*

9.5 Gourmet Crab Cakes

Yield:
4 servings

Prep time:
15 minutes

Cook time:
10 minutes

Ingredients:

- 1 pound lump crab meat, carefully picked over for shells
- 1/4 cup almond flour
- 1/4 cup mayonnaise
- 1 egg, beaten
- 2 tablespoons green onions, finely chopped
- 1 teaspoon Dijon mustard
- 1 teaspoon Worcestershire sauce
- 1/2 teaspoon Old Bay seasoning
- Salt and pepper to taste

Directions:

1. In a large bowl, combine the crab meat, almond flour, mayonnaise, beaten egg, green onions, Dijon mustard, Worcestershire sauce, Old Bay seasoning, salt, and pepper. Gently mix until well combined.
2. Form the mixture into 8 equal-sized cakes. If the mixture is too wet, you can add a little more almond flour to help it hold together.
3. Preheat the air fryer to 400°F.
4. Place the crab cakes in the basket in a single layer, making sure they are not touching. Spray the tops of the crab cakes lightly with olive oil spray.
5. Cook for 10 minutes, flipping halfway through or until the crab cakes are golden brown and heated through.
6. Serve immediately with lemon wedges and your favorite keto-friendly sauce if desired.

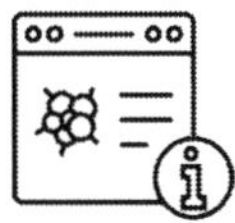

Nutritional Information: *230 calories, 24g protein, 4g carbohydrates, 15g fat, 2g fiber, 105mg cholesterol, 700mg sodium, 300mg potassium.*

9.6 Lemony Garlic Salmon Feast

Yield:
4 servings

Prep time:
10 minutes

Cook time:
12 minutes

Ingredients:

- 4 salmon fillets (about 6 ounces each)
- 2 tablespoons unsalted butter, melted
- 1 tablespoon olive oil
- 2 garlic cloves, minced
- Juice of 1 lemon
- 1 teaspoon lemon zest
- Salt and pepper to taste
- Fresh dill or parsley for garnish

Directions:

1. In a small bowl, combine melted butter, olive oil, minced garlic, lemon juice, and lemon zest. Season with salt and pepper to taste.
2. Preheat the air fryer to 400°F. Brush each salmon fillet with the lemon garlic butter mixture, ensuring all sides are coated.
3. Place the salmon fillets in the air fryer basket, skin-side down, making sure they do not touch.
4. Cook for 12 minutes or until the salmon is cooked through and flakes easily with a fork. The cooking time may vary depending on the thickness of the fillets.
5. 5. Serve immediately, garnished with fresh dill or parsley and additional lemon wedges if desired.

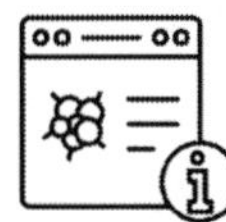

Nutritional Information: *280 calories, 23g protein, 0g carbohydrates, 20g fat, 0g fiber, 75mg cholesterol, 300mg sodium, 550mg potassium.*

9.7 Simple & Flavorful Tilapia

Yield:
4 servings

Prep time:
5 minutes

Cook time:
10 minutes

Ingredients:

- 4 tilapia fillets (about 6 ounces each)
- 2 tablespoons olive oil
- 1 teaspoon garlic powder
- 1 teaspoon paprika
- Salt and pepper to taste
- Lemon wedges for serving

Directions:

1. In a small bowl, mix together the olive oil, garlic powder, paprika, salt, and pepper.
2. Brush each tilapia fillet with the olive oil mixture, ensuring all sides are well coated.
3. Preheat the air fryer to 400°F. Place the tilapia fillets in the air fryer basket in a single layer, making sure they are not touching.
4. Cook for 10 minutes or until the tilapia is opaque and flakes easily with a fork. Depending on the thickness of your fillets, cooking time may need to be adjusted.
5. Serve immediately with lemon wedges on the side.

Nutritional Information: *180 calories, 23g protein, 0g carbohydrates, 10g fat, 0g fiber, 85mg cholesterol, 65mg sodium, 350mg potassium.*

9.8 Garlic Butter Lobster Tails

Yield:
4 servings

Prep time:
10 minutes

Cook time:
8 minutes

Ingredients:

- 4 lobster tails (5 to 6 ounces each)
- 4 tablespoons unsalted butter
- 1 clove garlic, minced
- 1 tablespoon fresh parsley, chopped
- 1 teaspoon lemon zest
- Salt and pepper to taste
- Lemon wedges for serving

Directions:

1. Preheat the air fryer to 380°F. Using kitchen shears, cut down the center of the top shell of each lobster tail, being careful not to cut through the lobster meat. Gently pry the shells apart and lift the tail meat, leaving it attached at the end. Rest the meat on top of the shells.
2. In a small saucepan, melt the butter over low heat. Add the minced garlic and cook until fragrant, about 1 minute. Remove from heat and stir in the chopped parsley, lemon zest, salt, and pepper.
3. Brush each lobster tail with the garlic butter mixture, making sure to cover both the meat and the shell. Place the lobster tails in the air fryer basket, meat side up. Cook for about 7-8 minutes or until the lobster meat is opaque and cooked through.
4. 4. Serve immediately with additional garlic butter and lemon wedges on the side.

Nutritional Information: *173 calories, 20g protein, 1g carbohydrates, 10g fat, 0g fiber, 143mg cholesterol, 293mg sodium, 349mg potassium.*

9.9 Lemon Butter Sea Scallops

Yield:
4 servings

Prep time:
5 minutes

Cook time:
5 minutes

Ingredients:

- 1 pound sea scallops, patted dry
- 2 tablespoons unsalted butter, melted
- 1 tablespoon olive oil
- Zest of 1 lemon
- 2 tablespoons lemon juice
- 1 garlic clove, minced
- Salt and pepper to taste
- Fresh parsley, chopped, for garnish

Directions:

1. In a small bowl, whisk together melted butter, olive oil, lemon zest, lemon juice, minced garlic, salt, and pepper. Toss the scallops in this mixture until they are well coated.
2. Preheat the air fryer to 400°F. Arrange the scallops in the air fryer basket in a single layer, ensuring they are not touching.
3. Cook for 5 minutes or until the scallops are opaque and cooked through. You may need to adjust the cooking time based on the size of your scallops.
4. Serve immediately, garnished with fresh parsley and additional lemon wedges on the side if desired.

Nutritional Information: *198 calories, 23g protein, 3g carbohydrates, 11g fat, 0g fiber, 56mg cholesterol, 414mg sodium, 468mg potassium.*

9.10 Zesty Catfish Fillets

Yield:
4 servings

Prep time:
10 minutes

Cook time:
10 minutes

Ingredients:

- 4 catfish fillets (about 6 ounces each)
- 1 tablespoon olive oil
- 1 teaspoon paprika
- 1 teaspoon garlic powder
- 1 teaspoon onion powder
- 1/2 teaspoon cayenne pepper (adjust to taste)
- Salt and black pepper to taste
- Lemon wedges for serving

Directions:

1. 1. In a small bowl, combine olive oil, paprika, garlic powder, onion powder, cayenne pepper, salt, and black pepper. Rub this mixture evenly over both sides of the catfish fillets.
2. 2. Preheat the air fryer to 400°F. Arrange the catfish fillets in the air fryer basket, ensuring they do not overlap.
3. 3. Cook for 10 minutes, flipping the fillets halfway through the cooking time or until the catfish is golden brown and flakes easily with a fork.
4. 4. Serve immediately with lemon wedges on the side.

Nutritional Information: *220 calories, 21g protein, 1g carbohydrates, 14g fat, 0g fiber, 85mg cholesterol, 70mg sodium, 450mg potassium.*

9.11 Light & Fresh Fish Tacos

Yield:
4 servings

Prep time:
15 minutes

Cook time:
10 minutes

Ingredients:

- 1 pound white fish fillets (e.g., cod, tilapia)
- 1 tablespoon olive oil
- 1 teaspoon chili powder
- 1 teaspoon cumin
- 1/2 teaspoon garlic powder
- 1/4 teaspoon salt
- 1/4 teaspoon black pepper
- 8 keto tortillas (store-bought or homemade)
- 1 avocado, sliced
- 1/4 cup shredded cabbage
- 1/4 cup sour cream
- 1 lime, cut into wedges
- Fresh cilantro for garnish (optional)

Directions:

1. Preheat the air fryer to 400°F. In a small bowl, mix together the chili powder, cumin, garlic powder, salt, and pepper. Rub the spice mixture all over the fish fillets and drizzle with olive oil.
2. Place the fish in the air fryer basket and cook for 10 minutes or until the fish is cooked through and flakes easily with a fork. Halfway through cooking, flip the fish to ensure even cooking.
3. Warm the keto tortillas according to the package instructions or by placing them in the air fryer for 1-2 minutes.
4. Break the cooked fish into pieces and assemble the tacos by placing fish, avocado slices, shredded cabbage, and a dollop of sour cream on each tortilla. Serve with lime wedges and garnish with fresh cilantro, if desired.

Nutritional Information: *350 calories, 25g protein, 9g carbohydrates, 23g fat, 5g fiber, 55mg cholesterol, 390mg sodium, 450mg potassium*

• •

9.12 Parmesan & Almond Crusted Calamari

Yield:
4 servings

Prep time:
10 minutes

Cook time:
8 minutes

Ingredients:

- 1 pound calamari, cleaned and cut into rings
- 1/2 cup almond flour
- 1/4 cup grated Parmesan cheese
- 1 teaspoon paprika
- 1/2 teaspoon garlic powder
- 1/4 teaspoon salt
- 1/4 teaspoon black pepper
- 1 egg

Directions:

1. In a shallow bowl, mix together the almond flour, grated Parmesan cheese, paprika, garlic powder, salt, and black pepper.
2. In another shallow bowl, beat the egg.
3. Dip each calamari ring first in the beaten egg and then coat it with the almond flour mixture. Make sure each ring is well-coated.
4. Place the coated calamari rings in the air fryer basket in a single layer. Spray lightly with olive oil spray. You may need to cook in batches to avoid overcrowding.
5. Air fry at 400°F for 8 minutes or until the calamari is golden and crispy. Halfway through cooking, flip the calamari rings to ensure even cooking.

Nutritional Information: *230 calories, 28g protein, 6g carbohydrates, 11g fat, 2g fiber, 264mg cholesterol, 340mg sodium, 370mg potassium.*

9.13 Mediterranean-Style Sardines

 Yield: **4 servings**

 Prep time: **10 minutes**

 Cook time: **10 minutes**

Ingredients:

- 1 pound fresh sardines, cleaned and gutted
- 1 tablespoon olive oil
- 1 teaspoon garlic powder
- 1 teaspoon smoked paprika
- 1/2 teaspoon salt
- 1/4 teaspoon black pepper
- 1 lemon, sliced for serving (optional)
- Fresh parsley, chopped for garnish (optional)

Directions:

1. Preheat your air fryer to 400°F.
2. In a large bowl, mix olive oil, garlic powder, smoked paprika, salt, and black pepper. Add the sardines and toss until they are evenly coated with the seasoning mix.
3. Arrange the sardines in a single layer in the air fryer basket. You may need to cook them in batches, depending on the size of your air fryer.
4. Cook for 10 minutes, flipping halfway through or until the sardines are golden and crispy.
5. Serve hot, garnished with lemon slices and chopped parsley if desired.

Nutritional Information: *200 calories, 24g protein, 0g carbohydrates, 12g fat, 0g fiber, 85mg cholesterol, 340mg sodium, 350mg potassium.*

9.14 Spiced Mackerel Fillets

 Yield: **4 servings**

 Prep time: **15 minutes**

 Cook time: **10 minutes**

Ingredients:

- 4 mackerel fillets, fresh or thawed
- 2 tablespoons olive oil
- 1 teaspoon garlic powder
- 1 teaspoon paprika
- Salt and pepper to taste
- 1 lemon, sliced for garnish
- Fresh parsley, chopped for garnish

Directions:

1. Preheat your air fryer to 400°F.
2. Rinse the mackerel fillets and pat them dry with paper towels. In a small bowl, mix together the olive oil, garlic powder, paprika, salt, and pepper.
3. Brush the spice mixture onto both sides of each mackerel fillet. Arrange the fillets in the air fryer basket, ensuring they are not touching for even cooking.
4. Cook in the air fryer for 10 minutes or until the mackerel is cooked through and flakes easily with a fork. Cooking times may vary depending on the thickness of the fillets and the type of air fryer used.
5. Serve immediately, garnished with lemon slices and chopped parsley.

Nutritional Information: *230 calories, 24g protein, 0g carbohydrates, 14g fat, 0g fiber, 95mg cholesterol, 105mg sodium, 520mg potassium.*

9.15 Spicy Citrus Shrimp

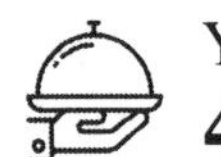

Yield: **4 servings**

Prep time: **10 minutes**

Cook time: **8 minutes**

Ingredients:

- 1 pound large shrimp, peeled and deveined
- 2 tablespoons olive oil
- 1 teaspoon garlic powder
- 1 teaspoon smoked paprika
- 1/2 teaspoon cayenne pepper (adjust according to spice preference)
- 1/2 teaspoon salt
- 1/4 teaspoon black pepper
- 1 tablespoon lemon juice
- Fresh parsley, chopped for garnish

Directions:

1. In a large bowl, combine olive oil, garlic powder, smoked paprika, cayenne pepper, salt, black pepper, and lemon juice. Mix well.
2. Add the shrimp to the bowl and toss until they are evenly coated with the seasoning mix.
3. Preheat the air fryer to 400°F for 5 minutes.
4. Place the shrimp in the air fryer basket in a single layer, ensuring they are not overlapping for even cooking.
5. Cook for 8 minutes or until the shrimp are pink and cooked through. You may need to shake the basket halfway through cooking for even crispiness.
6. Serve immediately, garnished with fresh parsley.

Nutritional Information: *200 calories, 24g protein, 1g carbohydrates, 12g fat, 0g fiber, 180mg cholesterol, 470mg sodium, 220mg potassium.*

Chapter 10:

Vegetables and Sides

10.1 Roasted Brussels Sprouts

Yield:
4 servings

Prep time:
10 minutes

Cook time:
15 minutes

Ingredients:

- 1 pound Brussels sprouts, trimmed and halved
- 2 tablespoons olive oil
- 1/2 teaspoon salt
- 1/4 teaspoon black pepper
- 1/4 teaspoon garlic powder
- 1/4 teaspoon onion powder
- 2 tablespoons grated Parmesan cheese (optional for garnish)

Directions:

1. In a large bowl, toss the Brussels sprouts with olive oil, salt, pepper, garlic powder, and onion powder until they are evenly coated.
2. Preheat the air fryer to 400°F. Place the Brussels sprouts in the air fryer basket in a single layer, ensuring they are not touching for optimal airflow. You may need to cook in batches, depending on the size of your air fryer.
3. Cook for about 15 minutes or until the Brussels sprouts are crispy on the outside and tender on the inside, shaking the basket or stirring halfway through the cooking time to ensure even cooking.
4. If using, sprinkle the cooked Brussels sprouts with grated Parmesan cheese before serving.
5. 5. Serve immediately as a delicious and healthy low-carb side dish.

Nutritional Information: *110 calories, 4g protein, 10g carbohydrates, 7g fat, 4g fiber, 0mg cholesterol, 320mg sodium, 440mg potassium.*

• •

10.2 Spiced Cauliflower Steaks

Yield:
4 servings

Prep time:
10 minutes

Cook time:
20 minutes

Ingredients:

- 1 large head cauliflower
- 2 tablespoons olive oil
- 1 teaspoon garlic powder
- 1 teaspoon smoked paprika
- 1/2 teaspoon salt
- 1/4 teaspoon black pepper
- Fresh parsley, chopped (for garnish)

Directions:

1. Remove the leaves from the cauliflower and cut the stem so that the cauliflower can sit flat. Slice the cauliflower into 4 steaks, approximately 1-inch thick.
2. In a small bowl, mix together olive oil, garlic powder, smoked paprika, salt, and pepper. Brush both sides of each cauliflower steak with the olive oil mixture.
3. Preheat the air fryer to 400°F. Place the cauliflower steaks in the air fryer basket in a single layer; you may need to cook them in batches, depending on the size of your air fryer.
4. Cook for 10 minutes, then flip the steaks and cook for an additional 10 minutes or until they are golden brown and tender. Garnish with chopped parsley before serving.

Nutritional Information: *107 calories, 3g protein, 8g carbohydrates, 7g fat, 4g fiber, 0mg cholesterol, 298mg sodium, 320mg potassium.*

10.3 Zucchini Fritters

Yield:
4 servings

Prep time:
15 minutes

Cook time:
10 minutes

Ingredients:

- 2 medium zucchinis, grated and excess moisture squeezed out
- 1 large egg
- 1/2 cup almond flour
- 1/4 cup grated Parmesan cheese
- 1/2 teaspoon garlic powder
- 1/2 teaspoon onion powder
- Salt and pepper to taste

Directions:

1. In a large bowl, combine grated zucchini, egg, almond flour, Parmesan cheese, garlic powder, onion powder, salt, and pepper. Mix well until all ingredients are thoroughly combined.
2. Preheat the air fryer to 400°F.
3. Form the zucchini mixture into small patties about the size of a burger. Place the patties in the air fryer basket in a single layer, making sure they do not touch.
4. Cook for 10 minutes, flipping the fritters halfway through the cooking time until they are golden brown and crispy.
5. Serve hot, with your choice of dipping sauce or as a side dish.

Nutritional Information: *155 calories, 9g protein, 8g carbohydrates, 11g fat, 4g fiber, 47mg cholesterol, 200mg sodium, 340mg potassium.*

10.4 Garlic-Infused Mushroom Bites

Yield:
4 servings

Prep time:
5 minutes

Cook time:
10 minutes

Ingredients:

- 1 pound button mushrooms, cleaned and stems removed
- 3 tablespoons olive oil
- 2 cloves garlic, minced
- 1/2 teaspoon salt
- 1/4 teaspoon black pepper
- 1 tablespoon fresh parsley, chopped (for garnish)

Directions:

1. In a large bowl, combine the mushrooms, olive oil, minced garlic, salt, and pepper. Toss well to ensure all the mushrooms are evenly coated.
2. Preheat the air fryer to 380°F. Place the mushrooms in the air fryer basket in a single layer. Depending on the size of your air fryer, you may need to cook them in batches.
3. Cook for 10 minutes, shaking the basket halfway through to ensure even cooking.
4. Transfer the mushrooms to a serving dish and garnish with fresh parsley. Serve immediately.

Nutritional Information: *107 calories, 3g protein, 4g carbohydrates, 9g fat, 1g fiber, 0mg cholesterol, 295mg sodium, 318mg potassium.*

10.5 Crispy Daikon Fries

 Yield: **4 servings**

 Prep time: **10 minutes**

Cook time: **15 minutes**

Ingredients:

- 1 large daikon radish, peeled and cut into fries
- 2 tablespoons avocado oil
- 1 teaspoon garlic powder
- 1/2 teaspoon paprika
- Salt and pepper to taste
- 1 tablespoon fresh parsley, chopped (for garnish)

Directions:

1. Toss the daikon fries with avocado oil, garlic powder, paprika, salt, and pepper in a bowl until they are evenly coated.
2. Preheat the air fryer to 400°F. Place the daikon fries in the air fryer basket in a single layer, making sure they are not overcrowded.
3. Cook for about 15 minutes, shaking the basket halfway through the cooking time, until the fries are golden brown and crispy.
4. Transfer to a serving plate and garnish with fresh parsley. Serve immediately.

Nutritional Information: *60 calories, 1g protein, 4g carbohydrates, 4.5g fat, 2g fiber, 0mg cholesterol, 45mg sodium, 270mg potassium.*

10.6 Parmesan Herb Spaghetti Squash

 Yield: **4 servings**

 Prep time: **10 minutes**

 Cook time: **30 minutes**

Ingredients:

- 1 medium spaghetti squash (about 2 pounds)
- 1 tablespoon olive oil
- 1 teaspoon salt
- 1/2 teaspoon black pepper
- 1/2 teaspoon garlic powder
- 1/4 teaspoon onion powder
- 1/4 cup grated Parmesan cheese (optional for serving)
- Fresh herbs (optional for serving)

Directions:

1. Preheat the air fryer to 400°F. Cut the spaghetti squash in half lengthwise and scoop out the seeds. Brush the inside of each half with olive oil and season with salt, pepper, garlic powder, and onion powder.
2. Place the squash halves in the air fryer basket cut side up. Cook for 30 minutes or until the flesh is tender and easily shreds with a fork.
3. Remove the squash from the air fryer, let it cool for a few minutes, then use a fork to scrape out the "spaghetti" strands into a bowl. Serve hot, topped with grated Parmesan cheese and fresh herbs, if desired.

Nutritional Information: *102 calories, 2g protein, 17g carbohydrates, 4g fat, 4g fiber, 4mg cholesterol, 593mg sodium, 260mg potassium.*

10.7 Spiced Roast Green Beans

Yield:
4 servings

Prep time:
10 minutes

Cook time:
15 minutes

Ingredients:

- 1 pound fresh green beans, trimmed
- 2 tablespoons olive oil
- 1/2 teaspoon garlic powder
- 1/2 teaspoon onion powder
- Salt and pepper to taste
- 1/4 teaspoon red pepper flakes (optional, for a bit of heat)

Directions:

1. In a large bowl, toss the green beans with olive oil, garlic powder, onion powder, salt, pepper, and red pepper flakes until evenly coated.
2. Preheat the air fryer to 400°F. Arrange the green beans in the air fryer basket in a single layer; you may need to do this in batches, depending on the size of your air fryer.
3. Cook in the preheated air fryer for about 12 to 15 minutes or until the green beans are roasted to your liking, shaking the basket halfway through cooking.
4. Serve immediately.

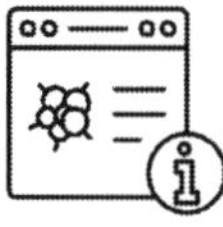

Nutritional Information: *87 calories, 2g protein, 10g carbohydrates, 5g fat, 4g fiber, 0mg cholesterol, 6mg sodium, 239mg potassium.*

10.8 Fiery Roasted Broccoli

Yield:
4 servings

Prep time:
10 minutes

Cook time:
12 minutes

Ingredients:

- 1 pound broccoli florets
- 2 tablespoons olive oil
- 1/4 teaspoon garlic powder
- 1/4 teaspoon onion powder
- 1/2 teaspoon chili flakes
- Salt and pepper to taste
- 1 tablespoon grated Parmesan cheese (optional, for garnishing)

Directions:

1. In a large bowl, combine the broccoli florets with olive oil, garlic powder, onion powder, chili flakes, salt, and pepper. Toss well to ensure the florets are evenly coated.
2. Preheat the air fryer to 400°F. Place the seasoned broccoli florets in the air fryer basket in a single layer, ensuring they are not overcrowded to allow for even cooking.
3. Cook for about 12 minutes or until the broccoli is tender and slightly crispy on the edges, shaking the basket halfway through cooking.
4. If desired, sprinkle the cooked broccoli with grated Parmesan cheese before serving.

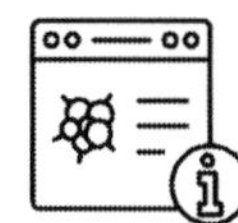

Nutritional Information: *114 calories, 3g protein, 8g carbohydrates, 8g fat, 3g fiber, 1mg cholesterol, 30mg sodium, 358mg potassium*

10.9 Creamy Spinach Bake

Yield:
4 servings

Prep time:
10 minutes

Cook time:
15 minutes

Ingredients:

- 10 ounces fresh spinach, washed and dried
- 1/2 cup heavy cream
- 4 ounces cream cheese, softened
- 1/2 cup grated Parmesan cheese
- 2 cloves garlic, minced
- 1/4 teaspoon nutmeg
- Salt and pepper to taste
- 1 tablespoon olive oil

Directions:

1. Preheat the air fryer to 380°F. In a large bowl, combine the spinach, heavy cream, cream cheese, Parmesan cheese, garlic, nutmeg, salt, and pepper. Mix well until all the ingredients are evenly incorporated.
2. Transfer the spinach mixture to a baking dish that fits in your air fryer. Drizzle the top with olive oil.
3. Place the dish in the air fryer and cook for about 15 minutes or until the mixture is bubbly and the top is slightly golden.
4. Carefully remove it from the air fryer and let it sit for a couple of minutes before serving.

Nutritional Information: *290 calories, 9g protein, 5g carbohydrates, 26g fat, 2g fiber, 85mg cholesterol, 390mg sodium, 450mg potassium.*

10.10 Cinnamon-Scented Butternut Squash

Yield:
4 servings

Prep time:
15 minutes

Cook time:
20 minutes

Ingredients:

- 1 medium butternut squash (about 2 pounds), peeled, seeded, and cut into 1/2-inch cubes
- 2 tablespoons olive oil
- 1 teaspoon ground cinnamon
- 1/2 teaspoon salt
- 1/4 teaspoon ground black pepper
- 1/4 teaspoon nutmeg

Directions:

1. In a large bowl, toss the butternut squash cubes with olive oil, cinnamon, salt, black pepper, and nutmeg until evenly coated.
2. Preheat the air fryer to 400°F. Arrange the squash in the air fryer basket in a single layer, working in batches if necessary to avoid overcrowding.
3. Cook for 20 minutes, shaking the basket halfway through the cooking time, until the squash is tender and golden brown.

Nutritional Information: *123 calories, 1.5g protein, 15g carbohydrates, 7g fat, 2.5g fiber, 0mg cholesterol, 298mg sodium, 430mg potassium.*

10.11 Parmesan Crusted Cabbage Steaks

Yield:
4 servings

Prep time:
10 minutes

Cook time:
15 minutes

Ingredients:

- 1 large head of cabbage, cut into 4 thick slices
- 2 tablespoons olive oil
- 1 teaspoon garlic powder
- 1 teaspoon paprika
- Salt and pepper to taste
- 1/4 cup grated Parmesan cheese (optional, for serving)

Directions:

1. Preheat the air fryer to 375°F. Brush both sides of each cabbage steak with olive oil, then season with garlic powder, paprika, salt, and pepper.
2. Place the cabbage steaks in the air fryer basket, making sure they are not overlapping. Cook for 15 minutes, flipping halfway through or until the edges are crispy and the center is tender.
3. Serve hot, optionally sprinkled with grated Parmesan cheese.

Nutritional Information: *114 calories, 3g protein, 9g carbohydrates, 7g fat, 4g fiber, 4mg cholesterol, 212mg sodium, 247mg potassium.*

10.12 Eggplant Mini Pizzas

Yield:
4 servings

Prep time:
10 minutes

Cook time:
10 minutes

Ingredients:

- 1 large eggplant, sliced into 1/2-inch thick rounds
- 2 tablespoons olive oil
- Salt and pepper to taste
- 1/2 cup low-carb pizza sauce (check the label for sugar content)
- 1 cup shredded mozzarella cheese
- 1/4 cup grated Parmesan cheese
- Toppings of choice (pepperoni, mushrooms, bell peppers, etc.)

Directions:

1. Preheat the air fryer to 400°F. Brush both sides of each eggplant round with olive oil, then season with salt and pepper.
2. Place the eggplant rounds in the air fryer basket in a single layer, working in batches if necessary. Cook for 5 minutes.
3. Flip the eggplant rounds, then spoon a small amount of pizza sauce onto each round. Top with mozzarella, Parmesan, and any other toppings of your choice.
4. Cook for another 5 minutes or until the cheese is melted and bubbly.

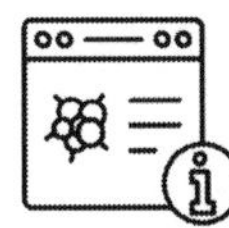

Nutritional Information: *190 calories, 9g protein, 8g carbohydrates, 14g fat, 4g fiber, 20mg cholesterol, 410mg sodium, 340mg potassium.*

Chapter 11:

Vegetarian Mains

Chapter 11 Fotos

11.1 Italian Cheese & Sun-Dried Tomato Avocados

Yield:
4 servings

Prep time:
15 minutes

Cook time:
10 minutes

Ingredients:

- 2 large avocados, halved and pitted
- 1/2 cup ricotta cheese
- 1/4 cup sun-dried tomatoes (not in oil), finely chopped
- 1/4 cup shredded mozzarella cheese
- 2 tablespoons pine nuts
- 1 tablespoon fresh basil, chopped
- 1/4 teaspoon garlic powder
- Salt and pepper to taste
- 1/4 cup grated Parmesan cheese for topping

Directions:

1. Preheat the air fryer to 350°F. Scoop out a bit of the avocado flesh to create more space for the filling, leaving a border around the edges. Chop the removed avocado flesh and set aside.
2. In a bowl, mix the ricotta cheese, sun-dried tomatoes, mozzarella cheese, pine nuts, basil, garlic powder, and chopped avocado. Season with salt and pepper to taste.
3. Fill each avocado half with the cheese mixture, and sprinkle the top with grated Parmesan cheese.
4. Place the stuffed avocados in the air fryer basket. Cook for 8-10 minutes or until the cheese is melted and bubbly.
5. 5. Serve warm, garnished with additional basil if desired.

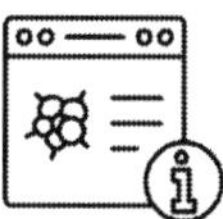

Nutritional Information: *290 calories, 10g protein, 12g carbohydrates, 24g fat, 7g fiber, 35mg cholesterol, 320mg sodium, 690mg potassium.*

11.2 Portobello Pizzas

Yield:
4 servings

Prep time:
15 minutes

Cook time:
8 minutes

Ingredients:

- 4 large Portobello mushroom caps, stems removed
- 1 tablespoon olive oil
- 1/2 teaspoon salt
- 1/4 teaspoon black pepper
- 1 cup marinara sauce (low-carb, sugar-free)
- 1 cup shredded mozzarella cheese
- 1/2 cup cherry tomatoes, halved
- 1/4 cup black olives, sliced
- 2 tablespoons fresh basil, chopped
- 1/4 teaspoon garlic powder
- 1/4 teaspoon dried oregano

Directions:

1. Preheat the air fryer to 375°F. Brush the Portobello mushroom caps with olive oil and season with salt and pepper.
2. Spoon marinara sauce into each mushroom cap, spreading it evenly. Top with shredded mozzarella cheese, cherry tomatoes, and black olives.
3. Sprinkle garlic powder and dried oregano over the top.
4. Place the stuffed mushroom caps in the air fryer basket. Cook for 8 minutes or until the cheese is melted and bubbly.
5. Garnish with fresh basil before serving.

Nutritional Information: *165 calories, 9g protein, 10g carbohydrates, 11g fat, 3g fiber, 22mg cholesterol, 587mg sodium, 512mg potassium.*

11.3 Tofu Nuggets

 Yield: **4 servings**

 Prep time: **15 minutes**

 Cook time: **15 minutes**

Ingredients:

- 1 block (14 oz) extra-firm tofu, pressed and drained
- 1/2 cup almond flour
- 1 tablespoon nutritional yeast
- 1 teaspoon garlic powder
- 1/2 teaspoon paprika
- 1/2 teaspoon salt
- 1/4 teaspoon black pepper
- 1 large egg, beaten (for a vegan option, use flaxseed meal mixed with water)
- Olive oil spray

Directions:

1. Cut the tofu into 1-inch cubes. Set aside.
2. In a shallow bowl, mix together almond flour, nutritional yeast, garlic powder, paprika, salt, and pepper.
3. Dip each tofu cube into the beaten egg, then coat with the almond flour mixture.
4. Place the coated tofu cubes in the air fryer basket. Spray lightly with olive oil.
5. Cook at 400°F for 15 minutes, turning halfway through, until the nuggets are golden and crispy.
6. Serve hot with your favorite low-carb dipping sauce.

Nutritional Information: *175 calories, 14g protein, 6g carbohydrates, 12g fat, 3g fiber, 53mg cholesterol, 320mg sodium, 200mg potassium.*

11.4 Layered Eggplant and Lentil Bake

 Yield: **4 servings**

 Prep time: **25 minutes**

 Cook time: **25 minutes**

Ingredients:

- 1 large eggplant, sliced into 1/2-inch thick rounds
- 1 cup cooked lentils
- 1 cup ricotta cheese
- 1/4 cup grated Parmesan cheese
- 1 cup shredded mozzarella cheese
- 1 cup low-carb marinara sauce
- 1 egg, beaten
- 1 tablespoon Italian seasoning
- 1 teaspoon garlic powder
- Salt and pepper to taste

Directions:

1. Preheat the air fryer to 375°F. In a bowl, mix together ricotta cheese, Parmesan cheese, beaten egg, Italian seasoning, garlic powder, salt, and pepper.
2. Spray both sides of the eggplant slices with olive oil and season with salt and pepper. Arrange the slices in a single layer in the air fryer basket and cook for 10 minutes, flipping halfway through until slightly tender.
3. On each eggplant slice, spread a spoonful of marinara sauce, then a layer of the ricotta mixture, some cooked lentils, and sprinkle with mozzarella cheese. Repeat layering until all ingredients are used.
4. Cook in the air fryer at 375°F for another 10 minutes or until the cheese is melted and bubbly.
5. Allow the lasagna to rest for a few minutes before serving.

Nutritional Information: *360 calories, 25g protein, 32g carbohydrates, 18g fat, 10g fiber, 90mg cholesterol, 780mg sodium, 670mg potassium.*

11.5 Cauliflower Mac and Cheese

Yield:
4 servings

Prep time:
15 minutes

Cook time:
20 minutes

Ingredients:

- 1 large head cauliflower, cut into small florets
- 1 tablespoon olive oil
- Salt and pepper, to taste
- 1 cup heavy cream
- 1 1/2 cups shredded cheddar cheese
- 1/4 cup grated Parmesan cheese
- 1/2 teaspoon garlic powder
- 1/2 teaspoon mustard powder
- 1/4 teaspoon cayenne pepper (optional)

Directions:

1. Preheat your air fryer to 375°F. In a large bowl, toss the cauliflower florets with olive oil, salt, and pepper. Place the cauliflower in the air fryer basket and cook for 12-15 minutes, shaking the basket halfway through, until the cauliflower is tender and starting to brown.
2. In a saucepan over medium heat, combine heavy cream, cheddar cheese, Parmesan cheese, garlic powder, mustard powder, and cayenne pepper. Cook, stirring constantly, until the cheese has melted and the sauce is smooth.
3. Pour the cheese sauce over the cooked cauliflower florets and toss to coat evenly. Transfer the coated cauliflower back into the air fryer basket. Cook for an additional 5 minutes at 375°F until the cheese is bubbly and beginning to brown.
4. Serve immediately.

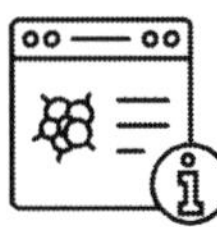

Nutritional Information: *475 calories, 18g protein, 12g carbohydrates, 40g fat, 3g fiber, 122mg cholesterol, 540mg sodium, 650mg potassium.*

11.6 Creamy Mushroom

Yield:
4 servings

Prep time:
15 minutes

Cook time:
20 minutes

Ingredients:

- 1 pound button mushrooms, sliced
- 1 small onion, finely chopped
- 2 cloves garlic, minced
- 1 cup vegetable broth
- 1/2 cup heavy cream
- 1/4 cup sour cream
- 2 tablespoons olive oil
- 1 tablespoon Worcestershire sauce (make sure it's vegetarian)
- 1 teaspoon Dijon mustard
- 1/4 teaspoon smoked paprika
- Salt and pepper to taste
- 2 tablespoons fresh parsley, chopped (for garnish)
- 1/4 cup grated Parmesan cheese (for serving)

Directions:

1. Preheat your air fryer to 380°F. In a bowl, mix the mushrooms with olive oil, garlic, salt, and pepper. Transfer the mushrooms to the air fryer basket and cook for 10 minutes, shaking the basket halfway through.
2. While the mushrooms are cooking, in a saucepan over medium heat, add the onion, garlic, and a splash of vegetable broth. Sauté until the onion is translucent, about 5 minutes.
3. Add the cooked mushrooms, remaining vegetable broth, heavy cream, sour cream, Worcestershire sauce, Dijon mustard, smoked paprika, salt, and pepper to the saucepan. Stir well to combine. Cook over low heat, stirring occasionally, until the sauce thickens, about 10 minutes.
4. Serve the mushroom stroganoff garnished with chopped parsley and grated Parmesan cheese.

Nutritional Information: *295 calories, 7g protein, 8g carbohydrates, 25g fat, 2g fiber, 41mg cholesterol, 310mg sodium, 450mg potassium.*

11.7 Zucchini Boats

 Yield: **4 servings**

Prep time: **15 minutes**

 Cook time: **10 minutes**

Ingredients:

- 1 block (14 oz) extra-firm tofu, 4 medium zucchinis, halved lengthwise and seeds scooped out
- 1 cup ricotta cheese
- 1/2 cup shredded mozzarella cheese
- 1/4 cup grated Parmesan cheese
- 1 cup chopped spinach
- 1/2 cup chopped mushrooms
- 1/2 teaspoon garlic powder
- 1/2 teaspoon Italian seasoning
- Salt and pepper to taste
- 1 tablespoon olive oil

Directions:

1. In a mixing bowl, combine ricotta cheese, mozzarella cheese, Parmesan cheese, chopped spinach, chopped mushrooms, garlic powder, Italian seasoning, salt, and pepper. Mix well until all ingredients are thoroughly combined.
2. Brush the inside of each zucchini boat with olive oil. Then, evenly distribute the cheese and vegetable mixture among the zucchini boats, pressing the mixture down gently into each zucchini.
3. Preheat the air fryer to 375°F. Place the stuffed zucchini boats in the air fryer basket in a single layer. You may need to cook them in batches, depending on the size of your air fryer.
4. Air fry for 10 minutes or until the zucchini is tender and the cheese is melted and lightly browned on top.

Nutritional Information: *220 calories, 14g protein, 8g carbohydrates, 15g fat, 2g fiber, 35mg cholesterol, 320mg sodium, 450mg potassium.*

11.8 Ricotta and Spinach Stuffed Peppers

 Yield: **4 servings**

Prep time: **20 minutes**

 Cook time: **15 minutes**

Ingredients:

- 4 large bell peppers, tops cut off and seeds removed
- 1 cup ricotta cheese
- 1 cup fresh spinach, chopped
- 1/2 cup shredded mozzarella cheese
- 1/4 cup grated Parmesan cheese
- 1 clove garlic, minced
- 1/2 teaspoon salt
- 1/4 teaspoon black pepper
- 1/4 teaspoon red pepper flakes (optional)
- 1 tablespoon olive oil

Directions:

1. In a bowl, combine ricotta cheese, chopped spinach, mozzarella cheese, Parmesan cheese, minced garlic, salt, black pepper, and red pepper flakes if using. Mix until all ingredients are well incorporated.
2. Fill each bell pepper with the ricotta and spinach mixture, pressing down gently to ensure the peppers are filled to capacity.
3. Brush the outside of each stuffed pepper with olive oil. This will help the peppers to cook evenly and get a nice color in the air fryer.
4. Preheat the air fryer to 350°F. Place the stuffed peppers in the air fryer basket, ensuring they are not touching to allow for even air circulation.
5. Air fry for 15 minutes or until the peppers are tender and the filling is heated through and slightly golden on top.

Nutritional Information: *250 calories, 15g protein, 9g carbohydrates, 18g fat, 3g fiber, 45mg cholesterol, 550mg sodium, 500mg potassium.*

11.9 Veggie Burger Patties

Yield: **4 servings**

Prep time: **15 minutes**

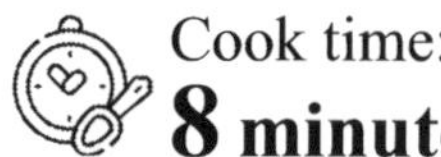
Cook time: **8 minutes**

Ingredients:

- 1 cup cauliflower rice, cooked and cooled
- 1 cup almond flour
- 1/2 cup shredded cheddar cheese
- 1/4 cup finely chopped bell pepper
- 1/4 cup finely chopped onion
- 2 large eggs
- 1 tablespoon psyllium husk powder (for binding)
- 1 teaspoon garlic powder
- 1 teaspoon smoked paprika
- Salt and pepper to taste

Directions:

1. In a large bowl, combine cauliflower rice, almond flour, cheddar cheese, bell pepper, onion, eggs, psyllium husk powder, garlic powder, smoked paprika, salt, and pepper. Mix thoroughly until the mixture is well combined and can hold together.
2. Form the mixture into four equal-sized patties.
3. Preheat the air fryer to 375°F. Lightly spray the air fryer basket with olive oil spray to prevent sticking.
4. Place the patties in the air fryer basket, making sure they are not touching to allow for even cooking. You may need to cook them in batches, depending on the size of your air fryer.
5. Air fry for 8 minutes, flipping the patties halfway through the cooking time until they are golden brown and cooked through.
6. Serve the keto veggie burger patties on low-carb buns or wrapped in lettuce leaves with your favorite toppings.

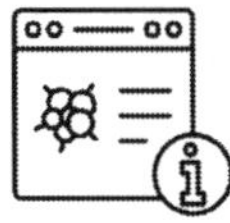

Nutritional Information: *280 calories, 14g protein, 10g carbohydrates, 20g fat, 6g fiber, 110mg cholesterol, 320mg sodium, 300mg potassium.*

11.10 Asparagus and Feta Tart

Yield: **4 servings**

Prep time: **10 minutes**

Cook time: **15 minutes**

Ingredients:

- 1 large low-carb tortilla or low-carb flatbread
- 1 tablespoon olive oil
- 1 garlic clove, minced
- 1/2 pound asparagus, trimmed and cut into 3-inch pieces
- 1/2 cup crumbled feta cheese
- Salt and pepper to taste
- 1/4 teaspoon red pepper flakes (optional)
- Fresh lemon zest, for garnish (optional)

Directions:

1. Preheat the air fryer to 350°F. Brush the low-carb tortilla or flatbread with olive oil and spread the minced garlic over the surface.
2. Arrange the asparagus pieces evenly over the tortilla, and sprinkle the crumbled feta cheese on top. Season with salt, pepper, and red pepper flakes if using.
3. Place the prepared tart in the air fryer basket. Air fry for 15 minutes or until the edges of the tortilla are golden brown and crispy and the asparagus is tender.
4. Remove the tart from the air fryer and let it cool for a couple of minutes. Garnish with fresh lemon zest if desired before serving.

Nutritional Information: *160 calories, 7g protein, 10g carbohydrates, 11g fat, 4g fiber, 25mg cholesterol, 420mg sodium, 250mg potassium.*

11.11 Herbal Falafel

Yield:
4 servings

Prep time:
15 minutes

Cook time:
10 minutes

Ingredients:

- 1 cup almond flour
- 2 cups canned chickpeas, drained and rinsed (for a keto version, you can substitute with cauliflower or zucchini for lower carbs)
- 1/4 cup fresh parsley, chopped
- 1/4 cup fresh cilantro, chopped
- 3 cloves garlic, minced
- 1 small onion, finely chopped
- 1 teaspoon ground cumin
- 1 teaspoon ground coriander
- 1/2 teaspoon salt
- 1/4 teaspoon black pepper
- 1/4 teaspoon cayenne pepper (optional for extra heat)
- 1 egg, beaten
- 2 tablespoons olive oil

Directions:

1. In a food processor, combine almond flour, chickpeas (or cauliflower/zucchini), parsley, cilantro, garlic, onion, cumin, coriander, salt, black pepper, and cayenne pepper. Pulse until the mixture is finely ground and starts to clump together.
2. Transfer the mixture to a bowl and mix in the beaten egg. This will help the falafel mixture bind together.
3. Form the mixture into small balls or patties, about 1 to 1.5 inches in diameter.
4. Preheat the air fryer to 370°F. Brush the falafel balls or patties with olive oil on all sides.
5. Place the falafel in the air fryer basket in a single layer, making sure they are not touching. You may need to cook in batches depending on the size of your air fryer.
6. Cook for 10 minutes, flipping halfway through or until the falafel is golden brown and crispy.
7. Serve hot with your choice of keto-friendly dipping sauce.

Nutritional Information (approximate, may vary based on substitutions):
320 calories, 14g protein, 10g carbohydrates, 25g fat, 6g fiber, 55mg cholesterol, 320mg sodium, 370mg potassium.

11.12 Cheesy Spinach Snack Balls

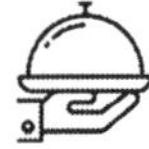
Yield:
4 servings

Prep time:
15 minutes

Cook time:
10 minutes

Ingredients:

- 2 cups fresh spinach, finely chopped
- 1 cup almond flour
- 1 cup shredded mozzarella cheese
- 1/2 cup grated Parmesan cheese
- 2 large eggs, beaten
- 1 teaspoon garlic powder
- 1/2 teaspoon salt
- 1/4 teaspoon ground black pepper

Directions:

1. In a large bowl, combine the chopped spinach, almond flour, mozzarella cheese, Parmesan cheese, beaten eggs, garlic powder, salt, and black pepper. Mix well until the mixture is uniform.
2. Form the mixture into small balls about the size of a golf ball. If the mixture is too sticky, you can wet your hands with a little water or olive oil to make it easier to handle.
3. Preheat your air fryer to 350°F.
4. Place the spinach balls in the basket in a single layer, making sure they are not touching. Work in batches if necessary.
5. Cook for 10 minutes or until the balls are golden and firm. You might want to shake the basket halfway through cooking to ensure even browning.
6. Serve hot, optionally, with a keto-friendly dipping sauce of your choice.

Nutritional Information: *320 calories, 18g protein, 8g carbohydrates, 24g fat, 4g fiber, 110mg cholesterol, 700mg sodium, 200mg potassium.*

Chapter 12:

Holiday Specials

Chapter 12 Fotos

12.1 Spiced Turkey Breast Feast

 Yield: **4 servings**

 Prep time: **10 minutes**

Cook time: **45 minutes**

Ingredients:

- 1 boneless turkey breast (approximately 2 pounds)
- 2 tablespoons olive oil
- 1 teaspoon salt
- 1/2 teaspoon black pepper
- 1 teaspoon garlic powder
- 1 teaspoon dried thyme
- 1 teaspoon dried rosemary
- 1/2 teaspoon smoked paprika

Directions:

1. Preheat your air fryer to 350°F. If your air fryer requires preheating, follow the manufacturer's instructions.
2. In a small bowl, mix together the olive oil, salt, black pepper, garlic powder, dried thyme, dried rosemary, and smoked paprika.
3. Rub the spice mixture all over the turkey breast, ensuring it is evenly coated.
4. Place the turkey breast in the air fryer basket. Make sure it fits nicely without touching the sides or the top of the air fryer.
5. Cook for approximately 45 minutes or until the internal temperature of the turkey breast reaches 165°F when checked with a meat thermometer.
6. Once cooked, remove the turkey breast from the air fryer and let it rest for 10 minutes before slicing. This helps retain the juices, making the turkey more flavorful and moist.
7. Slice and serve.

Nutritional Information (per serving): *250 calories, 35g protein, 0g carbohydrates, 12g fat, 0g fiber, 85mg cholesterol, 600mg sodium, 400mg potassium.*

12.2 Rosemary & Thyme Prime Rib

 Yield: **4 servings**

 Prep time: **5 minutes**

 Cook time: **50 minutes**

Ingredients:

- 1 prime rib roast (about 2 pounds)
- 2 tablespoons olive oil
- 1 tablespoon coarse sea salt
- 1 tablespoon freshly ground black pepper
- 2 teaspoons garlic powder
- 1 teaspoon dried rosemary
- 1 teaspoon dried thyme

Directions:

1. Let the prime rib roast come to room temperature for about 30 minutes before cooking.
2. Preheat your air fryer to 390°F. If your air fryer requires preheating, follow the manufacturer's instructions.
3. In a small bowl, mix together the olive oil, coarse sea salt, black pepper, garlic powder, dried rosemary, and dried thyme.
4. Rub the spice mixture all over the prime rib roast, ensuring it's evenly coated.
5. Place the prime rib in the air fryer basket, fat side up. Depending on the size of your air fryer, you may need to cut the roast to fit.
6. Cook for about 45-50 minutes for medium-rare, or adjust the time according to your preferred level of doneness. Use a meat thermometer to check the internal temperature: 120-125°F for rare, 130-135°F for medium-rare, and 140-145°F for medium.
7. Once cooked to your liking, remove the prime rib from the air fryer and let it rest for at least 10 minutes before slicing. This allows the juices to redistribute throughout the meat.
8. Slice and serve.

Nutritional Information (per serving): *520 calories, 45g protein, 0g carbohydrates, 38g fat, 0g fiber, 120mg cholesterol, 1760mg sodium, 600mg potassium.*

12.3 Glazed Ham

Yield:
4 servings

Prep time:
15 minutes

Cook time:
20 minutes

Ingredients:

- 2 pounds boneless ham (pre-cooked)
- 1/4 cup powdered erythritol
- 1 tablespoon Dijon mustard
- 1 teaspoon apple cider vinegar
- 1/2 teaspoon ground cinnamon
- 1/4 teaspoon ground cloves
- 1/4 teaspoon ground nutmeg
- 1/4 cup water

Directions:

1. In a small bowl, mix erythritol, Dijon mustard, apple cider vinegar, cinnamon, cloves, and nutmeg to create the glaze.
2. Place the ham in the air fryer basket and brush it with the glaze. Pour water into the bottom of the air fryer to prevent the glaze from burning.
3. Cook at 320°F for 10 minutes. Open the air fryer, brush the ham again with the glaze, and continue cooking for another 10 minutes or until the ham reaches an internal temperature of 140°F.
4. Let the ham rest for a few minutes before slicing. Serve warm.

Nutritional Information: *325 calories, 48g protein, 5g carbohydrates, 12g fat, 0g fiber, 120mg cholesterol, 2200mg sodium, 600mg potassium.*

12.4 Orange Aroma Duck Feast

Yield:
4 servings

Prep time:
20 minutes

Cook time:
60 minutes

Ingredients:

- 1 whole duck (approximately 5 to 6 pounds), defrosted if frozen
- 1 tablespoon sea salt
- 1/2 teaspoon black pepper
- 1 teaspoon garlic powder
- 1 teaspoon onion powder
- 1/2 teaspoon thyme
- 1 orange, quartered (for stuffing, optional)

Directions:

1. Pat the duck dry with paper towels. In a small bowl, mix the sea salt, black pepper, garlic powder, onion powder, and thyme. Rub the spice mixture all over the duck, inside and out.
2. If using, stuff the cavity of the duck with the quartered orange. This will add flavor and moisture but will not significantly affect the carb count, as you will not consume it.
3. Preheat your air fryer to 350°F (175°C). Place the duck breast side down in the air fryer basket. Cook for 30 minutes.
4. After 30 minutes, carefully flip the duck so it's breast side up. Continue cooking for an additional 30 minutes or until the skin is crispy and a meat thermometer inserted into the thickest part of the thigh reads 165°F (74°C).
5. Let the duck rest for 10 minutes before carving. This allows the juices to redistribute, making the meat moist and tender.

Nutritional Information: *1268 calories, 125g protein, 0g carbohydrates, 80g fat, 0g fiber, 326mg cholesterol, 3275mg sodium, 1385mg potassium.*

12.5 Creamy Green Bean & Mushroom Bake

Yield:
4 servings

Prep time:
15 minutes

Cook time:
20 minutes

Ingredients:

- 1 pound fresh green beans, trimmed and cut into bite-sized pieces
- 1 tablespoon olive oil
- 1/2 teaspoon salt
- 1/4 teaspoon black pepper
- 1 cup sliced mushrooms
- 2 cloves garlic, minced
- 1/2 cup heavy cream
- 1 cup shredded cheddar cheese
- 1/4 cup almond flour
- 1/4 cup grated Parmesan cheese
- 1 tablespoon butter, melted

Directions:

1. Preheat the air fryer to 375°F (190°C). In a large bowl, toss the green beans with olive oil, salt, and pepper. Transfer to the air fryer basket and cook for 10 minutes, shaking the basket halfway through.
2. While the green beans are cooking, sauté mushrooms and garlic in a skillet over medium heat until the mushrooms are soft, about 5 minutes. Stir in the heavy cream and bring to a simmer. Remove from heat and stir in the cheddar cheese until melted and smooth.
3. In a small bowl, mix together the almond flour, grated Parmesan cheese, and melted butter until the mixture resembles coarse crumbs.
4. Once the green beans are cooked, mix them with the mushroom and cheese sauce. Top with the almond flour mixture.
5. Return the basket to the air fryer and cook for another 10 minutes or until the topping is golden and crispy.
6. 6. Serve immediately.

Nutritional Information: *3350 calories, 12g protein, 10g carbohydrates, 29g fat, 4g fiber, 70mg cholesterol, 540mg sodium, 400mg potassium.*

12.6 Savory Almond Bread Stuffing

Yield:
4 servings

Prep time:
20 minutes

Cook time:
15 minutes

Ingredients:

- 4 cups almond flour bread (cubed and toasted)
- 1/2 cup celery (finely chopped)
- 1/4 cup onion (finely chopped)
- 1/4 cup butter
- 1 teaspoon sage (dried)
- 1 teaspoon thyme (dried)
- 1/2 teaspoon rosemary (dried)
- 1/2 teaspoon salt
- 1/4 teaspoon black pepper
- 1 cup chicken broth
- 2 eggs (beaten)

Directions:

1. Preheat your air fryer to 350°F (175°C). If you haven't already, cube your almond flour bread and toast the cubes lightly in the air fryer for about 5 minutes or until they're crispy. Remove and let cool.
2. In a skillet over medium heat, melt the butter. Add the celery and onion, and sauté until they are soft and translucent, about 5 minutes.
3. In a large bowl, combine the toasted almond flour bread cubes, sautéed celery and onion, sage, thyme, rosemary, salt, and pepper. Mix well.
4. In a small bowl, whisk together the chicken broth and beaten eggs. Pour this mixture over the bread mixture and stir until well combined. Let it sit for a few minutes so the bread can absorb the liquid.
5. Transfer the stuffing mixture to a baking dish that fits in your air fryer. Air fry at 350°F (175°C) for about 15 minutes or until the top is golden brown and crispy.
6. Serve hot as a side dish to your favorite keto main course.

Nutritional Information: *365 calories, 14g protein, 16g carbohydrates, 27g fat, 9g fiber, 120mg cholesterol, 700mg sodium, 135mg potassium.*

12.7 Asparagus with Blender Hollandaise

 Yield: **4 servings**

 Prep time: **10 minutes**

 Cook time: **8 minutes**

Ingredients:

- 1 pound fresh asparagus, ends trimmed
- 2 tablespoons olive oil
- Salt and pepper, to taste

For the Hollandaise Sauce:

- 3 egg yolks
- 1 tablespoon lemon juice
- 1/2 cup unsalted butter, melted
- Salt and cayenne pepper, to taste

Directions:

1. Preheat your air fryer to 400°F (200°C). In a large bowl, toss the asparagus with olive oil, salt, and pepper until evenly coated.
2. Place the asparagus in the air fryer basket in a single layer. You may need to cook in batches depending on the size of your air fryer. Cook for 8 minutes or until the asparagus is tender and slightly crispy on the ends.
3. While the asparagus is cooking, prepare the hollandaise sauce. In a blender, combine the egg yolks and lemon juice. Blend for about 10 seconds, then slowly add the melted butter while blending until the sauce thickens. Season with salt and cayenne pepper to taste.
4. Serve the roasted asparagus topped with the hollandaise sauce.

Nutritional Information: *295 calories, 3g protein, 3g carbohydrates, 31g fat, 2g fiber, 215mg cholesterol, 200mg sodium, 230mg potassium.*

12.8 Elegant Cranberry Brie Appetizers

 Yield: **4 servings**

 Prep time: **10 minutes**

 Cook time: **8 minutes**

Ingredients:

- 8 ounces Brie cheese, cut into 16 small pieces
- 1/2 cup homemade keto cranberry sauce (sugar-free)
- 16 almond flour crackers (store-bought or homemade for serving)
- A few sprigs of fresh rosemary for garnish (optional)

Directions:

1. Preheat your air fryer to 350°F (175°C). Cut the Brie cheese into 16 small pieces. If you're making homemade keto cranberry sauce, prepare it in advance.
2. Place the Brie pieces in the air fryer basket, ensuring they are not touching to prevent them from melting into each other. Cook for 4-5 minutes or until the Brie is just starting to melt and become gooey.
3. While the Brie is cooking, arrange the almond flour crackers on a serving platter.
4. Once the Brie is done, carefully remove each piece with a spatula and place it on top of an almond flour cracker. Top each Brie bite with a teaspoon of keto cranberry sauce.
5. Garnish with fresh rosemary sprigs if desired and serve immediately.

Nutritional Information: *200 calories, 12g protein, 6g carbohydrates, 15g fat, 2g fiber, 45mg cholesterol, 320mg sodium, 90mg potassium.*

12.9 Nutty Coconut Sweet Potato Bake

Yield:
4 servings

Prep time:
15 minutes

Cook time:
25 minutes

Ingredients:

- 2 medium-sized sweet potatoes, peeled and cubed
- 2 tablespoons olive oil
- 1/4 cup sweetener (erythritol or monk fruit)
- 1/2 teaspoon cinnamon
- 1/4 teaspoon nutmeg
- 1/4 cup chopped pecans (for topping)
- 1/4 cup shredded unsweetened coconut (for topping)
- Salt to taste

Directions:

1. Preheat your air fryer to 400°F (200°C). In a large bowl, toss the cubed sweet potatoes with olive oil, sweetener, cinnamon, nutmeg, and a pinch of salt until evenly coated.
2. Transfer the sweet potato mixture to an air fryer basket or tray, spreading them out in an even layer. Cook for 20 minutes, stirring halfway through or until the sweet potatoes are tender and starting to caramelize on the edges.
3. In the last 5 minutes of cooking, sprinkle the chopped pecans and shredded coconut over the sweet potatoes. Continue to cook until the topping is lightly toasted and the sweet potatoes are fully tender.
4. Serve warm as a low-carb side dish to your favorite main course.

Nutritional Information: *220 calories, 2g protein, 24g carbohydrates, 14g fat, 5g fiber, 0mg cholesterol, 110mg sodium, 360mg potassium.*

12.10 Pecan Pie Clusters

Yield:
4 servings

Prep time:
10 minutes

Cook time:
6 minutes

Ingredients:

- 1 cup pecans, roughly chopped
- 1/4 cup unsalted butter, melted
- 1/4 cup sugar-free maple syrup
- 1 teaspoon vanilla extract
- 1/4 teaspoon salt
- 2 tablespoons granulated erythritol (or another keto-friendly sweetener)
- 1/2 teaspoon cinnamon (optional)

Directions:

1. In a medium bowl, combine the chopped pecans, melted butter, sugar-free maple syrup, vanilla extract, salt, erythritol, and cinnamon (if using). Mix well to ensure all the pecans are evenly coated.
2. Preheat your air fryer to 350°F (175°C). Line the air fryer basket with parchment paper or a silicone liner to prevent sticking.
3. Spoon the pecan mixture into small clusters on the prepared basket, leaving some space between each for air circulation.
4. Cook for 6 minutes or until the clusters are golden and fragrant. Be careful not to let them burn.
5. Let the pecan pie clusters cool for a few minutes before removing them from the air fryer. They will continue to harden as they cool, creating a crunchy, sweet snack.
6. Serve and enjoy as a keto-friendly treat!

Nutritional Information: *220 calories, 2g protein, 4g carbohydrates, 22g fat, 3g fiber, 30mg cholesterol, 150mg sodium, 120mg potassium.*

12.11 Rosemary and Garlic Lamb Chops

Yield:
4 servings

Prep time:
15 minutes

Cook time:
10 minutes

Ingredients:

- 8 lamb chops
- 2 tablespoons olive oil
- 4 cloves garlic, minced
- 2 tablespoons fresh rosemary, finely chopped
- Salt and pepper to taste

Directions:

Marinade:

1. 1. In a large bowl, mix together olive oil, minced garlic, chopped rosemary, salt, and pepper. Add the lamb chops and toss until they are well coated with the marinade. Cover and refrigerate for at least 1 hour or overnight for best results.

Cooking Instructions:

1. Preheat your air fryer to 400°F (200°C).
2. Arrange the marinated lamb chops in the air fryer basket in a single layer. You may need to cook in batches depending on the size of your air fryer.
3. Cook for 10 minutes, flipping halfway through or until the lamb chops reach your desired level of doneness.
4. Let the lamb chops rest for a few minutes before serving. This allows the juices to redistribute throughout the meat, making it more tender and flavorful.
5. 5. Serve with a side of low-carb vegetables or a fresh salad for a complete keto-friendly meal.

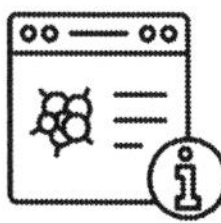

Nutritional Information: *Approximately 400 calories, 25g protein, 0g carbohydrates, 34g fat, 0g fiber, 105mg cholesterol, 75mg sodium, 315mg potassium.*

12.12 Brussels Sprouts with Crisp Bacon

Yield:
4 servings

Prep time:
10 minutes

Cook time:
15 minutes

Ingredients:

- 1 pound Brussels sprouts, trimmed and halved
- 4 slices of bacon, cut into small pieces
- 2 tablespoons olive oil
- Salt and pepper to taste
- 1 tablespoon balsamic vinegar (optional for a slight tang)

Directions:

1. Preheat your air fryer to 375°F (190°C). In a large bowl, toss the Brussels sprouts with the olive oil, salt, and pepper until they are well coated.
2. Add the bacon pieces to the bowl with the Brussels sprouts and toss to combine.
3. Transfer the Brussels sprouts and bacon mixture to the air fryer basket, spreading them out in an even layer.
4. Cook for about 15 minutes, shaking the basket halfway through the cooking time, until the Brussels sprouts are crispy on the edges and the bacon is cooked through.
5. If using, drizzle balsamic vinegar over the cooked Brussels sprouts and bacon before serving. Toss to coat evenly.
6. Serve hot as a delicious low-carb side dish.

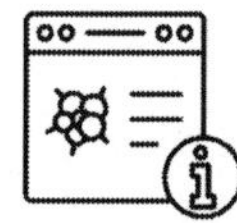

Nutritional Information: *220 calories, 10g protein, 10g carbohydrates, 16g fat, 4g fiber, 30mg cholesterol, 320mg sodium, 440mg potassium.*

12.13 Spiced Mixed Nuts

Yield:
4 servings

Prep time:
5 minutes

Cook time:
10 minutes

Ingredients:

- 2 cups mixed nuts (such as almonds, walnuts, pecans, and macadamias)
- 1 tablespoon olive oil
- 1 teaspoon ground cinnamon
- 1/2 teaspoon ground cumin
- 1/4 teaspoon cayenne pepper (adjust to taste)
- 1/2 teaspoon salt
- 1 tablespoon erythritol (or another keto-friendly sweetener)

Directions:

1. In a large bowl, combine the nuts with olive oil, cinnamon, cumin, cayenne pepper, salt, and erythritol. Toss well to ensure all the nuts are evenly coated with the spice mixture.
2. Preheat your air fryer to 350°F (175°C). Spread the spiced nuts in a single layer in the air fryer basket. Avoid overcrowding for even cooking.
3. Cook for 10 minutes, shaking the basket halfway through to ensure even cooking and to prevent the nuts from burning.
4. Remove the nuts from the air fryer and let them cool completely. They will crisp up as they cool.
5. Store in an airtight container at room temperature. Enjoy as a snack or add to salads and other dishes for extra texture and flavor.

Nutritional Information: *400 calories, 10g protein, 10g carbohydrates, 36g fat, 5g fiber, 0mg cholesterol, 300mg sodium, 300mg potassium.*

Chapter 13:

Delicious Desserts

Chapter 13 Fotos

13.1 Creamy Mini Cheesecakes

 Yield: **4 servings**

 Prep time: **20 minutes**

 Cook time: **15 minutes**

Ingredients:

- 1 cup almond flour
- 2 tablespoons unsalted butter, melted
- 1/4 cup erythritol
- 8 oz cream cheese, softened
- 1 large egg
- 1 teaspoon vanilla extract
- 1/4 cup sour cream
- Pinch of salt

Directions:

1. In a mixing bowl, combine almond flour, melted butter, and 1 tablespoon of erythritol. Press the mixture into the bottom of silicone muffin cups to form a base.
2. In another bowl, blend cream cheese, remaining erythritol, egg, vanilla extract, and sour cream until smooth. Spoon the filling over the crust in the muffin cups.
3. Place the filled muffin cups in the air fryer basket. Cook at 300°F for about 15 minutes or until the filling is set.
4. Allow to cool slightly before removing from the muffin cups. Chill in the refrigerator for at least 1 hour before serving.

Nutritional Information: *330 calories, 8g protein, 5g carbohydrates, 30g fat, 2g fiber, 90mg cholesterol, 160mg sodium, 200mg potassium.*

13.2 Chocolate Chip Cookies

 Yield: **4 servings**

 Prep time: **15 minutes**

 Cook time: **10 minutes**

Ingredients:

- 1 cup almond flour
- 1/4 cup coconut flour
- 1/2 teaspoon baking soda
- 1/4 teaspoon salt
- 1/3 cup unsalted butter, melted
- 1/4 cup erythritol (or another keto-friendly sweetener)
- 1 teaspoon vanilla extract
- 1 large egg
- 1/2 cup sugar-free chocolate chips

Directions:

1. In a medium bowl, whisk together almond flour, coconut flour, baking soda, and salt.
2. In another bowl, mix the melted butter, erythritol, vanilla extract, and egg until well combined.
3. Combine the wet ingredients with the dry ingredients and mix until a dough forms. Fold in the sugar-free chocolate chips.
4. Form the dough into small balls and flatten them slightly to form cookie shapes. Place cookies in the air fryer basket, making sure they do not touch.
5. Set the air fryer to 350°F and cook for about 10 minutes or until the cookies are golden and firm.

Nutritional Information: *210 calories, 6g protein, 8g carbohydrates, 18g fat, 3g fiber, 55mg cholesterol, 190mg sodium, 100mg potassium.*

13.3 Brownies

Yield:
4 servings

Prep time:
10 minutes

Cook time:
15 minutes

Ingredients:

- 1/2 cup almond flour
- 1/4 cup cocoa powder, unsweetened
- 1/3 cup granulated erythritol (or another keto-friendly sweetener)
- 1/4 teaspoon salt
- 1 teaspoon vanilla extract
- 2 large eggs
- 1/4 cup unsalted butter, melted
- 1/4 cup sugar-free chocolate chips

Directions:

1. In a medium mixing bowl, whisk together almond flour, cocoa powder, erythritol, and salt.
2. In another bowl, beat the eggs with the vanilla extract, then mix in the melted butter until well combined.
3. Combine the wet and dry ingredients until the batter is smooth. Fold in the chocolate chips.
4. Pour the batter into an air fryer-safe pan that fits your air fryer basket. Spread evenly.
5. Cook in the air fryer at 350°F for about 15 minutes or until a toothpick comes out clean. Allow to cool before cutting into pieces.

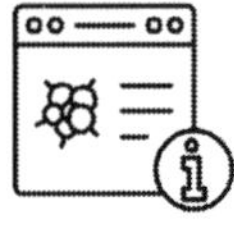

Nutritional Information: *215 calories, 6g protein, 9g carbohydrates, 19g fat, 4g fiber, 85mg cholesterol, 125mg sodium, 200mg potassium.*

13.4 Apple Fritters

Yield:
4 servings

Prep time:
15 minutes

Cook time:
10 minutes

Ingredients:

- 1 large apple, peeled, cored, and diced
- 1 cup almond flour
- 1/4 cup coconut flour
- 1 teaspoon baking powder
- 1/2 teaspoon cinnamon
- 1/4 teaspoon nutmeg
- Pinch of salt
- 2 tablespoons granulated erythritol (or another keto-friendly sweetener)
- 2 large eggs
- 1/4 cup unsweetened almond milk
- 1 teaspoon vanilla extract
- Coconut oil spray (for air fryer basket)

Directions:

1. In a mixing bowl, combine almond flour, coconut flour, baking powder, cinnamon, nutmeg, and salt.
2. In another bowl, whisk together eggs, almond milk, erythritol, and vanilla extract. Add the diced apples and stir until combined.
3. Gradually mix the wet ingredients into the dry ingredients until well combined. The batter should be thick.
4. Preheat the air fryer to 350°F. Spray the air fryer basket with coconut oil spray.
5. Spoon the batter into the air fryer basket in small fritter shapes, making sure they do not touch each other.
6. Cook for about 10 minutes, flipping halfway through, until the fritters are golden brown and cooked through.
7. Allow to cool slightly before serving.

Nutritional Information: *204 calories, 8g protein, 12g carbohydrates, 14g fat, 6g fiber, 93mg cholesterol, 186mg sodium, 134mg potassium.*

13.5 Almond Vanilla Donuts

Yield:
6 servings

Prep time:
15 minutes

Cook time:
10 minutes

Ingredients:

- 1 cup almond flour
- 1/4 cup coconut flour
- 1/3 cup granulated erythritol (or another keto-friendly sweetener)
- 1 teaspoon baking powder
- 1/2 teaspoon cinnamon
- Pinch of salt
- 2 large eggs
- 1/4 cup unsweetened almond milk
- 1/4 cup unsalted butter, melted
- 1 teaspoon vanilla extract
- Optional: sugar-free chocolate or glaze for topping

Directions:

1. In a mixing bowl, combine almond flour, coconut flour, erythritol, baking powder, cinnamon, and salt.
2. In another bowl, whisk together eggs, almond milk, melted butter, and vanilla extract.
3. Gradually mix the wet ingredients into the dry ingredients until well combined.
4. Form the dough into donut shapes using a donut mold or by making rings with your hands.
5. Preheat the air fryer to 350°F. Place the donuts in the air fryer basket, ensuring they do not touch.
6. Cook for about 10 minutes or until the donuts are golden and cooked through.
7. Allow to cool slightly, and apply optional toppings such as melted sugar-free chocolate or a keto-friendly glaze.

Nutritional Information: *205 calories, 6g protein, 10g carbohydrates, 17g fat, 4g fiber, 62mg cholesterol, 98mg sodium, 137mg potassium.*

13.6 Mixed Berry Crumble

Yield:
4 servings

Prep time:
10 minutes

Cook time:
15 minutes

Ingredients:

- 2 cups mixed berries (such as raspberries, blueberries, and blackberries), fresh or frozen
- 1 cup almond flour
- 1/4 cup granulated erythritol (or another keto-friendly sweetener)
- 1/4 cup unsalted butter, melted
- 1 teaspoon vanilla extract
- 1/2 teaspoon cinnamon
- Pinch of salt

Directions:

1. In a bowl, mix the berries with half of the erythritol and set aside.
2. In another bowl, combine the almond flour, the remaining erythritol, melted butter, vanilla extract, cinnamon, and salt. Mix until it forms a crumbly texture.
3. Place the berry mixture in an air fryer-safe dish that fits in the air fryer basket.
4. Sprinkle the crumbly almond flour mixture evenly over the berries.
5. Cook in the air fryer at 350°F for about 15 minutes or until the topping is golden brown and the berries are bubbling.
6. Allow to cool slightly before serving, as the berry mixture will be very hot.

Nutritional Information: *260 calories, 6g protein, 14g carbohydrates, 22g fat, 6g fiber, 31mg cholesterol, 5mg sodium, 130mg potassium.*

13.7 Pumpkin Cheesecake

 Yield: **4 servings**

 Prep time: **15 minutes**

 Cook time: **20 minutes**

Ingredients:

- 1 cup almond flour
- 2 tablespoons unsalted butter, melted
- 1/2 cup granulated erythritol (or another keto-friendly sweetener)
- 8 ounces cream cheese, softened
- 1/2 cup pumpkin puree
- 1 teaspoon vanilla extract
- 1 teaspoon pumpkin pie spice
- 1 large egg

Directions:

1. In a small bowl, combine almond flour, 1 tablespoon of erythritol, and melted butter. Press this mixture into the bottom of a small, air fryer-safe springform pan to form the crust.
2. In a mixing bowl, beat the cream cheese with the remaining erythritol until smooth. Add pumpkin puree, vanilla extract, pumpkin pie spice, and the egg, beating until well combined.
3. Pour the filling over the crust in the springform pan.
4. Cook in the air fryer at 300°F for 20 minutes or until the cheesecake is set but still slightly jiggly in the center.
5. Allow to cool in the pan before refrigerating for at least 4 hours, preferably overnight, to set completely.
6. Serve chilled.

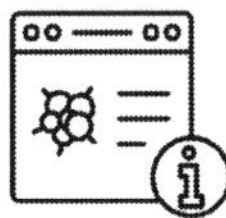

Nutritional Information: *320 calories, 8g protein, 10g carbohydrates, 29g fat, 3g fiber, 85mg cholesterol, 180mg sodium, 200mg potassium.*

• •

13.8 Zesty Lemon Squares

 Yield: **6 servings**

 Prep time: **15 minutes**

 Cook time: **12 minutes**

Ingredients:

- 1 cup almond flour
- 1/4 cup coconut flour
- 1/3 cup granulated erythritol (or another keto-friendly sweetener)
- 1/4 cup unsalted butter, melted
- 3 large eggs
- 1/2 cup fresh lemon juice
- Zest of 1 lemon
- 1/2 teaspoon vanilla extract
- Pinch of salt

Directions:

1. In a mixing bowl, combine almond flour, coconut flour, and a pinch of salt. Mix in melted butter until a crumbly dough forms.
2. Press the dough evenly into the bottom of an air fryer-safe baking dish that fits in your air fryer.
3. In another bowl, whisk together eggs, erythritol, lemon juice, lemon zest, and vanilla extract until smooth.
4. Pour the lemon mixture over the crust in the baking dish.
5. Cook in the air fryer at 300°F for 12 minutes or until the filling is set and the edges are slightly golden.
6. Let the lemon bars cool completely before cutting into squares.

Nutritional Information: *190 calories, 6g protein, 8g carbohydrates, 15g fat, 3g fiber, 106mg cholesterol, 45mg sodium, 102mg potassium.*

13.9 Coconut Macaroons

Yield:
4 servings

Prep time:
10 minutes

Cook time:
10 minutes

Ingredients:

- 2 cups unsweetened shredded coconut
- 1/3 cup granulated erythritol (or another keto-friendly sweetener)
- 2 large egg whites
- 1 teaspoon vanilla extract
- Pinch of salt

Directions:

1. In a bowl, mix together the shredded coconut, erythritol, and salt.
2. Stir in the egg whites and vanilla extract until well combined. The mixture should be sticky and hold together when squeezed.
3. Form the mixture into small, round mounds and place them on a parchment paper-lined air fryer basket, ensuring they do not touch each other.
4. Cook in the air fryer at 320°F for 10 minutes or until the macaroons are golden and firm.
5. Allow to cool for a few minutes before serving.

Nutritional Information: *280 calories, 3g protein, 10g carbohydrates, 25g fat, 7g fiber, 0mg cholesterol, 60mg sodium, 130mg potassium.*

• •

13.10 Vanilla Almond Cake

Yield:
4 servings

Prep time:
10 minutes

Cook time:
20 minutes

Ingredients:

- 1 cup almond flour
- 1/4 cup granulated erythritol
- 1 teaspoon baking powder
- 1/4 teaspoon salt
- 2 large eggs
- 1/4 cup unsalted butter, melted
- 1 teaspoon vanilla extract
- 2 tablespoons unsweetened almond milk

Directions:

1. In a mixing bowl, combine the almond flour, erythritol, baking powder, and salt.
2. Whisk in the eggs, melted butter, vanilla extract, and almond milk until the batter is smooth.
3. Pour the batter into a greased 6-inch cake pan that fits in your air fryer.
4. Set the air fryer to 320°F and cook the cake for 20 minutes or until a toothpick inserted into the center comes out clean.
5. Allow the cake to cool for a few minutes before removing it from the pan and serving.

Nutritional Information: *345 calories, 9g protein, 7g carbohydrates, 31g fat, 3g fiber, 115mg cholesterol, 220mg sodium, 90mg potassium.*

13.11 Decadent Chocolate Lava Cake

Yield:
2 servings

Prep time:
10 minutes

Cook time:
8 minutes

Ingredients:

- 2 ounces unsweetened baking chocolate
- 1/4 cup unsalted butter
- 1/4 cup granulated erythritol
- 1 large egg
- 1 teaspoon vanilla extract
- 1 tablespoon almond flour
- 1/4 teaspoon baking powder
- Pinch of salt
- Optional: 1 tablespoon heavy cream (for more richness)

Directions:

1. Melt the chocolate and butter together in a microwave-safe bowl or using a double boiler until smooth. Allow to cool slightly.
2. Stir in the erythritol, egg, and vanilla extract into the chocolate mixture until well combined.
3. Mix in the almond flour, baking powder, and salt until no lumps remain.
4. Divide the batter evenly between two greased ramekins or silicone molds that can fit in your air fryer.
5. Cook in the air fryer at 350°F for about 8 minutes or until the edges are set, but the center is still soft.
6. Let sit for 1-2 minutes before serving. Optionally, serve with a dollop of whipped cream or a sprinkle of powdered erythritol.

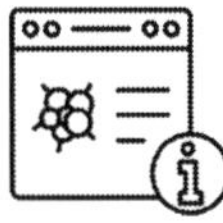

Nutritional Information: *398 calories, 6g protein, 8g carbohydrates, 38g fat, 4g fiber, 124mg cholesterol, 83mg sodium, 102mg potassium.*

13.12 Pecan Pie Mug Cake

Yield:
2 servings

Prep time:
5 minutes

Cook time:
10 minutes

Ingredients:

- 1/4 cup almond flour
- 2 tablespoons crushed pecans
- 1 tablespoon granulated erythritol
- 1/2 teaspoon baking powder
- 1/4 teaspoon ground cinnamon
- Pinch of salt
- 1 large egg
- 2 tablespoons unsalted butter, melted
- 1/2 teaspoon vanilla extract

Directions:

1. In a small bowl, mix together the almond flour, crushed pecans, erythritol, baking powder, cinnamon, and salt.
2. Add the egg, melted butter, and vanilla extract to the dry ingredients and stir until well combined.
3. Pour the batter into a microwave-safe mug or a small ramekin that fits in your air fryer.
4. Place the mug or ramekin in the air fryer and cook at 350°F for 10 minutes or until the cake is set and a toothpick inserted in the center comes out clean.
5. Allow the cake to cool slightly before eating. Serve warm.

Nutritional Information: *295 calories, 6g protein, 5g carbohydrates, 27g fat, 2g fiber, 106mg cholesterol, 95mg sodium, 130mg potassium.*

13.13 Nutty Almond Biscotti

Yield:
6 servings

Prep time:
15 minutes

Cook time:
20 minutes

Ingredients:

- 1 cup almond flour
- 1/3 cup granulated erythritol
- 1 teaspoon baking powder
- 1/4 teaspoon salt
- 2 large eggs
- 1 teaspoon vanilla extract
- 1/2 teaspoon almond extract
- 1/4 cup chopped almonds
- Optional: 1/4 cup sugar-free dark chocolate chips

Directions:

1. In a mixing bowl, combine almond flour, erythritol, baking powder, and salt.
2. In another bowl, whisk the eggs with vanilla and almond extracts until well blended.
3. Mix the wet ingredients into the dry ingredients until a dough forms. Fold in the chopped almonds and optional chocolate chips.
4. Form the dough into a log shape, approximately 8 inches long and 2 inches wide, on a baking sheet or foil that fits in the air fryer basket.
5. Air fry at 330°F for 12 minutes. Remove and let cool slightly, then cut into 1/2-inch thick slices.
6. Place the slices back in the air fryer and cook for an additional 8 minutes, flipping halfway through, until crisp and golden.
7. Allow to cool completely on a wire rack before serving. Store in an airtight container.

Nutritional Information: *160 calories, 6g protein, 5g carbohydrates, 14g fat, 3g fiber, 62mg cholesterol, 83mg sodium, 120mg potassium.*

13.14 Lemon Ricotta Bites

Yield:
4 servings

Prep time:
15 minutes

Cook time:
10 minutes

Ingredients:

- 1 cup whole milk ricotta cheese
- 1 large egg
- 1/4 cup almond flour
- 2 tablespoons granulated erythritol
- Zest of 1 lemon
- 1/4 teaspoon vanilla extract
- Pinch of salt
- Optional: 1/4 cup unsweetened shredded coconut for coating

Directions:

1. In a mixing bowl, combine the ricotta, egg, almond flour, erythritol, lemon zest, vanilla extract, and salt. Mix well until all ingredients are thoroughly combined.
2. Shape the mixture into small balls about 1 inch in diameter.
3. If using, roll the balls in shredded coconut to coat evenly.
4. Place the balls in the air fryer basket, making sure they are not touching to ensure even cooking.
5. Cook in the air fryer at 350°F for 10 minutes or until the balls are firm and slightly golden.
6. Serve warm or at room temperature.

Nutritional Information: *180 calories, 9g protein, 5g carbohydrates, 14g fat, 1g fiber, 75mg cholesterol, 125mg sodium, 100mg potassium.*

13.15 Simple Vanilla Flan

Yield:
4 servings

Prep time:
10 minutes

Cook time:
20 minutes

Ingredients:

- 1 cup heavy cream
- 1/2 cup unsweetened almond milk
- 1/3 cup granulated erythritol
- 3 large eggs
- 1 teaspoon vanilla extract
- Pinch of salt

Caramel Sauce:
- 1/4 cup granulated erythritol
- 1 tablespoon water
- 1/2 teaspoon lemon juice

Directions:

1. First, make the caramel sauce. In a small saucepan, combine the erythritol, water, and lemon juice. Heat over medium heat, stirring constantly, until the mixture becomes golden and syrupy. Pour into the bottom of four heat-resistant ramekins.
2. In a mixing bowl, whisk together the heavy cream, almond milk, erythritol, eggs, vanilla extract, and a pinch of salt until smooth.
3. Pour the cream mixture over the caramel in each ramekin.
4. Place the ramekins in the air fryer basket, ensuring they are not touching each other. Cook at 320°F for 20 minutes or until the flan is set but slightly jiggly in the center.
5. Remove from the air fryer and let cool at room temperature for about 15 minutes, then refrigerate for at least 2 hours before serving.

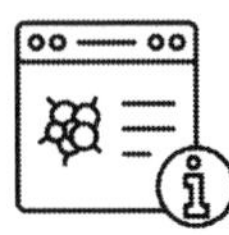

Nutritional Information: *280 calories, 6g protein, 3g carbohydrates, 26g fat, 0g fiber, 215mg cholesterol, 85mg sodium, 50mg potassium.*

13.16 Pumpkin Pie Cups

Yield:
4 servings

Prep time:
15 minutes

Cook time:
15 minutes

Ingredients:

- 1 cup almond flour
- 1/4 cup unsalted butter, melted
- 2 tablespoons erythritol (or another low-carb sweetener)
- 1 teaspoon vanilla extract
- 1/2 teaspoon cinnamon
- 1/4 teaspoon nutmeg
- 1/4 teaspoon ginger
- 1/4 teaspoon salt
- 1 cup canned pumpkin puree
- 1/2 cup heavy cream
- 2 large eggs
- Whipped cream (for topping, optional)

Directions:

1. In a medium bowl, mix the almond flour, melted butter, 1 tablespoon erythritol, vanilla extract, and a pinch of salt until a dough forms. Divide the dough into 4 equal portions and press into the bottom and sides of silicone muffin cups to form a crust.
2. In another bowl, combine the pumpkin puree, heavy cream, eggs, and the remaining 1 tablespoon of erythritol, cinnamon, nutmeg, ginger, and a pinch of salt. Whisk until smooth.
3. Pour the pumpkin mixture into the crusts, filling each about three-quarters full.
4. Preheat your air fryer to 350°F. Place the silicone muffin cups in the air fryer basket and cook for 15 minutes or until the filling is set and the edges are lightly golden.
5. Let cool for a few minutes before removing from the muffin cups. Serve warm or chilled, topped with whipped cream if desired.

Nutritional Information: *180 calories, 9g protein, 5g carbohydrates, 14g fat, 1g fiber, 75mg cholesterol, 125mg sodium, 100mg potassium.*

Chapter 14:

Keto Breads and Pastries

14.1 Almond Flour Bread

Yield:
4 servings

Prep time:
10 minutes

Cook time:
30 minutes

Ingredients:

- 1 1/2 cups almond flour
- 1/4 cup ground flaxseed
- 3 tablespoons coconut flour
- 1 teaspoon baking powder
- 1/4 teaspoon salt
- 4 large eggs
- 1/4 cup unsalted butter, melted
- 2 tablespoons sour cream
- 1 teaspoon apple cider vinegar

Directions:

1. In a large mixing bowl, combine almond flour, ground flaxseed, coconut flour, baking powder, and salt.
2. In another bowl, whisk together eggs, melted butter, sour cream, and apple cider vinegar.
3. Pour the wet ingredients into the dry ingredients and mix until well combined.
4. Transfer the batter to a greased, air fryer-friendly loaf pan.
5. Place the loaf pan in the air fryer and cook at 320°F for about 30 minutes or until a toothpick inserted into the center comes out clean.

Nutritional Information: *345 calories, 14 g protein, 8 g carbohydrates, 29 g fat, 5 g fiber, 215 mg cholesterol, 190 mg sodium, 134 mg potassium.*

14.2 Coconut Flour Muffins

Yield:
6 servings

Prep time:
15 minutes

Cook time:
20 minutes

Ingredients:

- 1/2 cup coconut flour
- 1/4 teaspoon salt
- 1/2 teaspoon baking powder
- 1/4 cup erythritol (or another keto-friendly sweetener)
- 4 large eggs
- 1/4 cup unsalted butter, melted
- 1/2 cup unsweetened almond milk
- 1 teaspoon vanilla extract

Directions:

1. In a medium bowl, whisk together the coconut flour, salt, baking powder, and erythritol.
2. In another bowl, beat the eggs and then mix in the melted butter, almond milk, and vanilla extract.
3. Combine the wet and dry ingredients until the batter is smooth.
4. Spoon the batter into muffin cups that fit your air fryer basket, filling each about three-quarters full.
5. Set the air fryer to 350°F and bake for about 20 minutes or until the tops are golden and a toothpick inserted into the center of a muffin comes out clean.

Nutritional Information: *180 calories, 6 g protein, 7 g carbohydrates, 15 g fat, 3 g fiber, 155 mg cholesterol, 125 mg sodium, 50 mg potassium.*

14.3 Easy Mozzarella Bagels

 Yield: **4 servings**

 Prep time: **10 minutes**

 Cook time: **12 minutes**

Ingredients:

- 1 1/2 cups almond flour
- 1 tablespoon ground psyllium husk
- 2 teaspoons baking powder
- 1/2 teaspoon garlic powder (optional)
- 1/2 teaspoon onion powder (optional)
- 1/4 teaspoon salt
- 2 large eggs
- 2 tablespoons apple cider vinegar
- 1/2 cup shredded mozzarella cheese
- Sesame seeds or everything bagel seasoning for topping

Directions:

1. In a large bowl, mix the almond flour, psyllium husk, baking powder, garlic powder, onion powder, and salt.
2. In another bowl, whisk together the eggs and apple cider vinegar.
3. Add the wet ingredients to the dry ingredients along with the mozzarella cheese and mix until a dough forms.
4. Divide the dough into 4 equal parts and shape each into a bagel form on a parchment-lined air fryer basket. Sprinkle with sesame seeds or everything bagel seasoning.
5. Air fry at 375°F for about 12 minutes or until golden and cooked through.

Nutritional Information: *320 calories, 15 g protein, 10 g carbohydrates, 25 g fat, 5 g fiber, 120 mg cholesterol, 290 mg sodium, 100 mg potassium.*

14.4 Cheese Danish

 Yield: **4 servings**

 Prep time: **15 minutes**

 Cook time: **10 minutes**

Ingredients:

- 1 cup almond flour
- 1/4 cup coconut flour
- 1 teaspoon baking powder
- 2 tablespoons erythritol (or another keto-friendly sweetener)
- 1 large egg
- 1/4 cup unsalted butter, melted
- 1 teaspoon vanilla extract
- 4 ounces cream cheese, softened
- 2 tablespoons powdered erythritol (for filling)
- 1 teaspoon lemon zest (optional for filling)

Directions:

1. In a mixing bowl, combine almond flour, coconut flour, baking powder, and 2 tablespoons of erythritol.
2. In a separate bowl, whisk together the egg, melted butter, and vanilla extract.
3. Combine the wet ingredients with the dry ingredients until a dough forms.
4. Divide the dough into four equal parts and flatten each into a small disc on a parchment-lined air fryer basket.
5. In another bowl, mix the softened cream cheese, powdered erythritol, and lemon zest until smooth.
6. Place a spoonful of the cream cheese mixture in the center of each dough disc.
7. Fold the edges of the dough slightly over the filling, leaving the center exposed.
8. Air fry at 350°F for about 10 minutes or until the edges are golden brown.

Nutritional Information: *320 calories, 10 g protein, 8 g carbohydrates, 28 g fat, 4 g fiber, 110 mg cholesterol, 200 mg sodium, 90 mg potassium.*

14.5 Cheesy Garlic Knots

 Yield: **4 servings**

 Prep time: **15 minutes**

 Cook time: **8 minutes**

Ingredients:

- 1 1/2 cups shredded mozzarella cheese
- 2 tablespoons cream cheese
- 1 cup almond flour
- 1 tablespoon coconut flour
- 1 teaspoon baking powder
- 1 large egg
- 1/4 cup grated Parmesan cheese
- 2 tablespoons olive oil
- 2 cloves garlic, minced
- 1 tablespoon chopped fresh parsley
- 1/2 teaspoon salt

Directions:

1. In a microwave-safe bowl, combine the mozzarella and cream cheese. Microwave for 1 minute, stir, and then heat for another 30 seconds until the cheese is fully melted.
2. In a separate bowl, mix together the almond flour, coconut flour, and baking powder.
3. Add the egg to the melted cheese mixture and mix well. Then, incorporate the flour mixture until a dough forms.
4. Divide the dough into 8 equal portions. Roll each portion into a 6-inch rope and then tie it into a knot.
5. In a small bowl, mix together olive oil, minced garlic, parsley, and salt.
6. 6. Brush the garlic mixture over the knots before placing them in the air fryer basket.
7. 7. Air fry at 375°F for about 8 minutes or until golden and set.

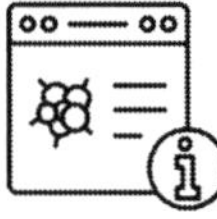

Nutritional Information: *300 calories, 18 g protein, 8 g carbohydrates, 23 g fat, 3 g fiber, 120 mg cholesterol, 460 mg sodium, 90 mg potassium.*

14.6 Simple Pretzels

 Yield: **4 servings**

Prep time: **15 minutes**

 Cook time: **10 minutes**

Ingredients:

- 1 1/2 cups shredded mozzarella cheese
- 2 tablespoons cream cheese
- 1 cup almond flour
- 1 tablespoon coconut flour
- 1 teaspoon xanthan gum (optional for texture)
- 1 large egg, beaten (reserve half for egg wash)
- 1/2 teaspoon garlic powder (optional)
- Coarse salt for sprinkling

Directions:

1. In a microwave-safe bowl, combine the mozzarella and cream cheese. Microwave for 1 minute, stir, and then microwave for another 30 seconds until the cheese is fully melted.
2. Stir in the almond flour, coconut flour, and xanthan gum until well combined.
3. Add half of the beaten egg (reserve the other half for egg wash) and mix until a dough forms.
4. Divide the dough into 4 equal parts. Roll each part into a long rope and then shape it into a pretzel form.
5. Brush the shaped pretzels with the remaining egg wash and sprinkle with coarse salt.
6. Place the pretzels in the air fryer basket, making sure they do not touch.
7. Air fry at 350°F for about 10 minutes or until golden brown.

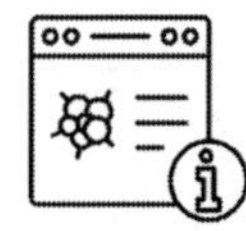

Nutritional Information: *280 calories, 18 g protein, 6 g carbohydrates, 22 g fat, 3 g fiber, 105 mg cholesterol, 430 mg sodium, 75 mg potassium.*

14.7 Zesty Zucchini Bread

Yield:
4 servings

Prep time:
15 minutes

Cook time:
25 minutes

Ingredients:

- 1 cup grated zucchini (excess moisture squeezed out)
- 1 1/2 cups almond flour
- 1/4 cup coconut flour
- 2 teaspoons baking powder
- 1/2 teaspoon salt
- 1/2 teaspoon cinnamon
- 3 large eggs
- 1/3 cup unsweetened almond milk
- 1/4 cup olive oil
- 1/4 cup erythritol (or another keto-friendly sweetener)
- 1 teaspoon vanilla extract

Directions:

1. In a large bowl, combine almond flour, coconut flour, baking powder, salt, and cinnamon.
2. In another bowl, whisk together eggs, almond milk, olive oil, erythritol, and vanilla extract.
3. Stir in the grated zucchini.
4. 4. Gradually mix the wet ingredients into the dry ingredients until well combined.
5. Transfer the batter to a greased, air fryer-safe baking pan.
6. Place the pan in the air fryer and cook at 320°F for about 25 minutes or until a toothpick inserted into the center comes out clean.

Nutritional Information: *280 calories, 12 g protein, 10 g carbohydrates, 23 g fat, 6 g fiber, 140 mg cholesterol, 330 mg sodium, 200 mg potassium.*

14.8 Pumpkin Bread

Yield:
4 servings

Prep time:
15 minutes

Cook time:
25 minutes

Ingredients:

- 1 cup almond flour
- 1/4 cup coconut flour
- 2 teaspoons baking powder
- 1 teaspoon ground cinnamon
- 1/2 teaspoon ground nutmeg
- 1/4 teaspoon ground cloves
- 1/4 teaspoon salt
- 1/2 cup pumpkin puree
- 1/4 cup unsalted butter, melted
- 3 large eggs
- 1/3 cup erythritol (or another keto-friendly sweetener)
- 1 teaspoon vanilla extract

Directions:

1. In a large bowl, combine almond flour, coconut flour, baking powder, cinnamon, nutmeg, cloves, and salt.
2. In another bowl, whisk together pumpkin puree, melted butter, eggs, erythritol, and vanilla extract.
3. Gradually mix the wet ingredients into the dry ingredients until well combined.
4. Transfer the batter to a greased, air fryer-safe baking pan.
5. Place the pan in the air fryer and cook at 325°F for about 25 minutes or until a toothpick inserted into the center comes out clean.

Nutritional Information: *260 calories, 10 g protein, 9 g carbohydrates, 21 g fat, 4 g fiber, 185 mg cholesterol, 300 mg sodium, 130 mg potassium.*

14.9 Blueberry Scones

Yield:
4 servings

Prep time:
15 minutes

Cook time:
12 minutes

Ingredients:

- 1 1/2 cups almond flour
- 1/4 cup coconut flour
- 1/3 cup erythritol (or another keto-friendly sweetener)
- 1 teaspoon baking powder
- 1/4 teaspoon salt
- 1/4 cup unsalted butter, cold and cubed
- 1/4 cup heavy cream
- 1 large egg
- 1/2 teaspoon vanilla extract
- 1/2 cup fresh blueberries

Directions:

1. In a large bowl, combine almond flour, coconut flour, erythritol, baking powder, and salt.
2. Add the cold, cubed butter to the flour mixture and use a pastry cutter or your fingers to blend until the mixture resembles coarse crumbs.
3. In a small bowl, whisk together the heavy cream, egg, and vanilla extract.
4. Stir the wet ingredients into the flour mixture until just combined, then gently fold in the blueberries.
5. Form the dough into a circle on a piece of parchment paper and cut into 4 wedges.
6. Transfer the wedges to the air fryer basket, spacing them apart.
7. Air fry at 350°F for about 12 minutes or until the scones are golden brown and cooked through.

Nutritional Information: *315 calories, 10 g protein, 12 g carbohydrates, 26 g fat, 5 g fiber, 115 mg cholesterol, 220 mg sodium, 90 mg potassium.*

14.10 Cheddar Biscuits

Yield:
4 servings

Prep time:
10 minutes

Cook time:
10 minutes

Ingredients:

- 1 cup almond flour
- 1/4 cup coconut flour
- 1 teaspoon baking powder
- 1/4 teaspoon garlic powder
- 1/4 teaspoon salt
- 1/2 cup shredded sharp cheddar cheese
- 1/4 cup unsalted butter, melted
- 2 large eggs
- 1 tablespoon heavy cream
- 1 tablespoon fresh chopped parsley (optional for garnish)

Directions:

1. In a large bowl, mix together almond flour, coconut flour, baking powder, garlic powder, and salt.
2. Stir in the shredded cheddar cheese.
3. In a separate bowl, whisk together melted butter, eggs, and heavy cream.
4. Combine the wet ingredients with the dry ingredients until a dough forms.
5. Divide the dough into four equal parts and form each into a biscuit shape.
6. Place the biscuits in the air fryer basket, ensuring they are not touching.
7. Air fry at 350°F for about 10 minutes or until they are golden brown and firm to the touch.
8. Optional: Garnish with fresh chopped parsley before serving.

Nutritional Information: *315 calories, 12 g protein, 8 g carbohydrates, 27 g fat, 4 g fiber, 115 mg cholesterol, 310 mg sodium, 100 mg potassium.*

14.11 Banana Walnut Bread

Yield:
4 servings

Prep time:
15 minutes

Cook time:
25 minutes

Ingredients:

- 1 cup almond flour
- 1/4 cup coconut flour
- 1 teaspoon baking powder
- 1/2 teaspoon cinnamon
- 1/4 teaspoon salt
- 1/2 cup crushed walnuts
- 1/4 cup unsalted butter, melted
- 2 large eggs
- 1/4 cup erythritol (or another keto-friendly sweetener)
- 1 teaspoon vanilla extract
- 2 teaspoons banana extract (to mimic banana flavor without the carbs)

Directions:

1. In a large bowl, combine almond flour, coconut flour, baking powder, cinnamon, and salt.
2. Stir in the crushed walnuts.
3. In another bowl, mix together the melted butter, eggs, erythritol, vanilla extract, and banana extract.
4. Gradually add the wet ingredients to the dry ingredients, stirring until well combined.
5. Transfer the batter to a greased, air fryer-safe baking pan.
6. Place the pan in the air fryer and cook at 320°F for about 25 minutes or until a toothpick inserted into the center comes out clean.

Nutritional Information: *310 calories, 10 g protein, 9 g carbohydrates, 27 g fat, 4 g fiber, 135 mg cholesterol, 200 mg sodium, 150 mg potassium.*

14.12 Mozzarella Croissants

Yield:
4 servings

Prep time:
20 minutes

Cook time:
12 minutes

Ingredients:

- 1 1/2 cups mozzarella cheese, shredded
- 2 ounces cream cheese
- 1 cup almond flour
- 1 tablespoon coconut flour
- 1 teaspoon baking powder
- 1 large egg (for the dough)
- 1 egg yolk (for egg wash)
- Optional: sesame seeds or poppy seeds for topping

Directions:

1. In a microwave-safe bowl, combine the mozzarella and cream cheese. Microwave for 1 minute, stir, and microwave for another 30 seconds until completely melted and smooth.
2. Add the almond flour, coconut flour, and baking powder to the melted cheese mixture, stirring well to combine.
3. Beat the egg and mix it into the dough until fully integrated.
4. Divide the dough into 4 equal parts. Roll each piece into a thin rectangle, then roll up tightly to form a croissant shape.
5. Place the croissants on a parchment paper-lined air fryer basket. Brush with egg yolk and sprinkle with optional seeds.
6. Air fry at 350°F for about 12 minutes or until golden and puffed up.

Nutritional Information: *330 calories, 18 g protein, 8 g carbohydrates, 26 g fat, 3 g fiber, 140 mg cholesterol, 320 mg sodium, 90 mg potassium.*

14.13 Pizza Crust

Yield:
2 servings

Prep time:
10 minutes

Cook time:
8 minutes

Ingredients:

- 1 cup almond flour
- 1/4 cup coconut flour
- 2 tablespoons ground flaxseed
- 1 teaspoon baking powder
- 1/2 teaspoon salt
- 2 large eggs
- 2 tablespoons olive oil
- 2 tablespoons water

Directions:

1. In a large mixing bowl, combine almond flour, coconut flour, ground flaxseed, baking powder, and salt.
2. In another bowl, whisk together eggs, olive oil, and water.
3. Pour the wet ingredients into the dry ingredients and stir until a dough forms.
4. Place the dough on a piece of parchment paper and press or roll it into a round pizza shape, about 1/4 inch thick.
5. Transfer the parchment with the dough onto the air fryer basket.
6. Air fry at 350°F for about 8 minutes or until the crust is golden and firm.
7. Remove the crust, add your favorite low-carb toppings, and return to the air fryer for an additional 2-3 minutes to melt the toppings.

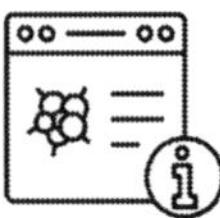

Nutritional Information: *320 calories, 12 g protein, 14 g carbohydrates, 25 g fat, 6 g fiber, 185 mg cholesterol, 300 mg sodium, 100 mg potassium.*

14.14 Cinnamon Rolls

Yield:
4 servings

Prep time:
20 minutes

Cook time:
10 minutes

Ingredients:

- 1 1/2 cups mozzarella cheese, shredded
- 2 ounces cream cheese
- 1 cup almond flour
- 1 tablespoon coconut flour
- 1 teaspoon baking powder
- 1 large egg
- 2 tablespoons erythritol (or another keto-friendly sweetener)
- 1 teaspoon cinnamon
- 2 tablespoons butter, melted (for filling)
- 2 tablespoons erythritol (additional for filling)
- 1 teaspoon vanilla extract (for icing)
- 2 tablespoons cream cheese (for icing)
- 2 tablespoons heavy cream (for icing)

Directions:

1. In a microwave-safe bowl, combine mozzarella and cream cheese. Microwave for 1 minute, stir, and microwave for an additional 30 seconds until fully melted.
2. Add almond flour, coconut flour, and baking powder to the cheese mixture and mix well.
3. Stir in the egg and erythritol to form a dough.
4. Roll out the dough between two pieces of parchment paper into a rectangle.
5. Brush the dough with melted butter, then sprinkle with additional erythritol and cinnamon.
6. Roll the dough tightly from the long edge to form a log.
7. Cut the log into 4 equal pieces and place them in the air fryer basket.
8. 8. Air fry at 350°F for about 10 minutes or until golden brown.
9. 9. For the icing, mix cream cheese, heavy cream, and vanilla extract until smooth. Drizzle over warm cinnamon rolls.

Nutritional Information: *350 calories, 14 g protein, 8 g carbohydrates, 30 g fat, 3 g fiber, 140 mg cholesterol, 320 mg sodium, 100 mg potassium.*

14.15 Focaccia

Yield:
4 servings

Prep time:
15 minutes

Cook time:
15 minutes

Ingredients:

- 1 1/2 cups almond flour
- 1/4 cup coconut flour
- 1 tablespoon psyllium husk powder
- 1 teaspoon baking powder
- 1/2 teaspoon salt
- 1/2 cup warm water
- 2 tablespoons olive oil (plus extra for drizzling)
- 1 large egg
- 1 tablespoon fresh rosemary, chopped
- 1/2 teaspoon garlic powder
- Coarse sea salt for sprinkling

Directions:

1. In a large mixing bowl, combine almond flour, coconut flour, psyllium husk powder, baking powder, and salt.
2. In another bowl, whisk together warm water, 2 tablespoons of olive oil, and the egg.
3. Gradually add the wet ingredients to the dry ingredients, stirring until a sticky dough forms.
4. Press the dough into a flat, even layer on a parchment-lined air fryer basket. It should be about 1/2 inch thick.
5. Drizzle additional olive oil over the top and sprinkle with chopped rosemary, garlic powder, and coarse sea salt.
6. Air fry at 350°F for about 15 minutes or until golden brown and firm to the touch.

Nutritional Information: *280 calories, 10 g protein, 12 g carbohydrates, 23 g fat, 6 g fiber, 95 mg cholesterol, 300 mg sodium, 150 mg potassium.*

Chapter 15:

Meal Plan Week

Welcome to the most exciting part of our keto journey together—the Meal Plan Week chapter! This isn't just any meal plan; it's your roadmap to a week full of flavor, fun, and the magic of your air fryer. Whether you're a keto newbie or a seasoned pro, I've got something special for everyone.

In this chapter, we take the guesswork out of "What's for dinner?"—and breakfast and lunch, too! I've laid out a full week's worth of meals designed to keep your taste buds tingling and your keto goals on track. You'll find easy-to-follow plans that cater to all sorts of lifestyles, from the bustling parent hustling between work, gym, and home to the adventurous foodie craving something new and delicious.

Each day is perfectly planned with meals that use recipes from our fabulous cookbook. I've linked them directly to their specific recipes so you can jump right to the page you need. No, flipping through pages wondering what to cook—it's all there at your fingertips!

Beginner

Beginner Keto Air Fryer User

- **Monday:** Breakfast - 4.1 Cheesy Omelet Toast; Lunch - 5.1 Aromatic Spiced Chicken Delight; Dinner - 9.1 Lemon Dill Salmon Elegance
- **Tuesday:** Breakfast - 4.8 Vanilla Berry Custard Toast; Lunch - 5.3 Crispy Almond-Crusted Mozzarella Bites; Dinner - 7.1 Italian Herb Chicken Parmesan
- **Wednesday:** Breakfast - 4.4 Spinach and Cheese Egg Muffins; Lunch - 5.6 Cheesy Stuffed Jalapenos; Dinner - 8.7 Beef & Cauliflower Rice Stuffed Peppers
- **Thursday:** Breakfast - 4.3 Cauliflower Crust Egg Muffins; Lunch - 4.2 Golden Harvest Granola; Dinner - 8.5 Tender Pork Belly Cubes
- **Friday:** Breakfast - 4.7 Bacon-Wrapped Egg Delights; Lunch - 5.5 Herb-Infused Salmon Patties; Dinner - 8.4 Savory Beef Stick Delights
- **Saturday:** Breakfast - 4.5 Cheesy Ham Omelet Cups; Lunch - 5.7 Italian-Style Beef Meatballs; Dinner - 9.9 Lemon Butter Sea Scallops
- **Sunday:** Breakfast - 4.10 Garden Veggie Egg Cups; Lunch - 4.21 Crispy Bacon Avocado Quarters; Dinner - 8.13 Rustic Sausage-Cabbage Medley

Intermediate Keto Air Fryer User

- **Monday:** Breakfast - 4.13 Cheesy Avocado Egg Nests; Lunch - 5.14 Savory Chicken Fingers; Dinner - 8.3 Rosemary-Infused Lamb Chops
- **Tuesday:** Breakfast - 4.14 Sausage and Cheddar Breakfast Muffins; Lunch - 5.2 Smoky Paprika Shrimp Sensation; Dinner - 9.12 Parmesan & Almond Crusted Calamari
- **Wednesday:** Breakfast - 4.15 Crispy Radish Hash Browns; Lunch - 5.12 Cheesy Zucchini Bites; Dinner - 9.3 Italian Herb Tuna Elegance
- **Thursday:** Breakfast - 4.17 Almond Flour Pancake Poppers; Lunch - 5.4 Spicy Buffalo Cauliflower Poppers; Dinner - 9.5 Gourmet Crab Cakes
- **Friday:** Breakfast - 4.19 Mediterranean Bliss Frittata; Lunch - 5.10 Parmesan Garlic Chicken Wings; Dinner - 9.2 Lemon Simplicity Cod
- **Saturday:** Breakfast - 4.16 Savory Scotch Delights; Lunch - 6.5 Fiesta-Style Low-Carb Nachos; Dinner - 8.12 Mushroom-Infused Stroganoff Balls
- **Sunday:** Breakfast - 4.18 Cinnamon Toast Sticks; Lunch - 6.7 Coconut Bliss Shrimp; Dinner - 7.7 Duck Breast Delight

Advanced Keto Air Fryer User

- **Monday:** Breakfast - 13.4 Apple Fritters; Lunch - 5.11 Almond-Crusted Tofu Delights; Dinner - 8.8 Classic Ribeye
- **Tuesday:** Breakfast - 13.1 Creamy Mini Cheesecakes; Lunch - 6.1 Savory Mushroom Delights; Dinner - 7.13 Spiced Chicken Tikka Bites
- **Wednesday:** Breakfast - 13.2 Chocolate Chip Cookies; Lunch - 6.12 Buffalo Chicken Creamy Delight; Dinner - 8.14 Tender Pulled Pork Perfection
- **Thursday:** Breakfast - 13.3 Brownies; Lunch - 6.10 Cauliflower Nuggets; Dinner - 8.2 Herb-Seasoned Pork Chops
- **Friday:** Breakfast - 13.5 Almond Vanilla Donuts; Lunch - 6.3 Savory Cheese Puffs; Dinner - 7.15 Keto Chicken Schnitzel
- **Saturday:** Breakfast - 13.6 Mixed Berry Crumble; Lunch - 6.6 Almond Parmesan Pickle Bites; Dinner - 8.10 Mint Lamb Meatballs
- **Sunday:** Breakfast - 13.7 Pumpkin Cheesecake; Lunch - 6.4 Avocado Bliss Fingers; Dinner - 8.11 Pork Carnitas with Lime

Expert Keto Air Fryer User

- **Monday:** Breakfast - 13.14 Lemon Ricotta Bites; Lunch - 8.1 Golden Keto Empanadas; Dinner - 9.6 Lemony Garlic Salmon Feast
- **Tuesday:** Breakfast - 13.10 Vanilla Almond Cake; Lunch - 8.6 Flavorful Beef Loaf; Dinner - 9.8 Garlic Butter Lobster Tails
- **Wednesday:** Breakfast - 13.11 Decadent Chocolate Lava Cake; Lunch - 10.2 Spiced Cauliflower Steaks; Dinner - 9.10 Zesty Catfish Filets
- **Thursday:** Breakfast - 13.12 Pecan Pie Mug Cake; Lunch - 11.1 Italian Cheese & Sun-Dried Tomato Avocados; Dinner - 9.7 Simple & Flavorful Tilapia
- **Friday:** Breakfast - 13.15 Simple Vanilla Flan; Lunch - 11.2 Portobello Pizzas; Dinner - 9.2 Lemon Simplicity Cod
- **Saturday:** Breakfast - 13.8 Zesty Lemon Squares; Lunch - 11.3 Tofu Nuggets; Dinner - 9.13 Mediterranean-Style Sardines
- **Sunday:** Breakfast - 13.16 Pumpkin Pie Cups; Lunch - 11.4 Layered Eggplant and Lentil Bake; Dinner - 9.14 Spiced Mackerel Fillets

Chapter 16:

Conclusion + Bonus

Key Takeaways

Wow, what a ride it's been! From the basics of the keto diet to mastering the air fryer, you've gained the knowledge and tools to transform your eating habits. Remember, the key is balance, using your air fryer to whip up meals that are not only nutritious but also irresistibly tasty. Let these recipes be a springboard for your creativity in the kitchen.

Sustaining Your Keto Journeyy

Keeping keto can seem daunting, but it's all about the long game. Set yourself up for success with meal prepping, regular grocery runs, and keeping your spice rack stocked. Small steps lead to big wins, and consistency is your best friend on this journey.

Success Stories

Hear from others who've transformed their lives with keto and an air fryer by their side. These stories aren't just about weight loss; they're about gaining a new zest for life, improved health, and a love for cooking. Let these tales inspire you to write your own success story.

Community and Support

You're not alone! The keto community is vast and incredibly supportive. Join online forums, attend local meet-ups, or start a keto blog. Sharing your journey can provide encouragement and accountability, plus you might just make some new friends along the way.

Further Learning

The world of keto is always evolving. Keep up with the latest research, books, podcasts, and articles to stay informed and inspired. Knowledge is power, and staying curious is key to keeping your diet exciting and effective.

The Joy of Keto Cooking

Discover the sheer joy of crafting meals that are as good for you as they are delicious. Experiment with flavors, textures, and ingredients to find what makes your taste buds sing. Cooking is not just about sustenance—it's about pleasure and sharing with those you love.

Adapting Keto to Your Lifestyle

Keto isn't one-size-fits-all. Whether you're a busy parent, a student, or someone who travels frequently, adapt the principles of keto to fit your life. Tailor your meal planning and preparation to suit your schedule and preferences.

Looking Ahead

What's next for you on this keto journey? Set new goals, whether they're related to health, fitness, or culinary achievements. Maybe you'll aim to master keto baking next, or perhaps you'll focus on growing your own herbs and vegetables. The possibilities are endless.

Words of Motivation

Lastly, remember why you started. Whether it's for health or fitness or simply to feel better in your daily life, keep those reasons close to your heart. Stay motivated, stay committed, and above all, enjoy every step of the journey.

I hope you've enjoyed diving into the world of keto cooking with your air fryer as much as I have loved sharing my favorite recipes with you!

But wait, there's more! Scan the QR code to unlock a special **bonus chapter** *featuring* **15 extraordinary and delicious sauces** *that will elevate your dishes to a whole new level.*

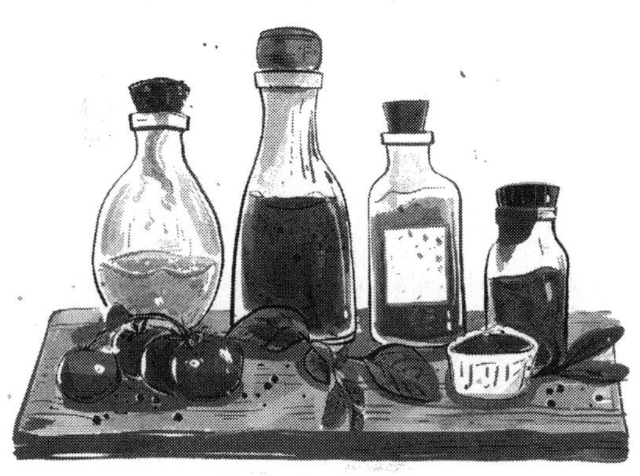

As a thank you for being a part of this journey, I kindly ask you to take a moment and leave a review of my book. Your feedback means the world to me and helps others discover the joys of keto cooking. Enjoy the bonus recipes, and happy cooking!

Please scan the QR code below to leave a review.

Chapter 17:

Appendix 1. Measurement Conversion Chart

Category	Metric	Imperial
Cup Volume	60 ml	1/4 cup
	80 ml	1/3 cup
	125 ml	1/2 cup
	250 ml	1 cup
Spoon Volume	1.25 ml	1/4 teaspoon
	2.5 ml	1/2 teaspoon
	5 ml	1 teaspoon
	20 ml	1 tablespoon
Mass (Weight)	10 g	1/4 oz
	15 g	1/2 oz
	30 g	1 oz
	250 g	8 oz (1/2 lb)
	500 g	16 oz (1 lb)
	1 kg	32 oz (2 lb)
Oven Temperature	80°C	170°F
	100°C	200°F
	120°C	250°F
	150°C	300°F
	180°C	350°F
	200°C	400°F
	220°C	450°F
	250°C	500°F

Chapter 18:

Appendix 2. Air Fryer Cooking Chart

In this appendix, you'll find a comprehensive air fryer cooking chart to guide you through the perfect cooking times and temperatures for a variety of keto-friendly foods. Whether you're crisping up bacon or roasting a succulent piece of chicken, this chart helps ensure that every meal you make is delicious and cooked to perfection.

Here's what a typical air fryer cooking chart includes:

Vegetables:

- Asparagus: 400°F for 5-7 minutes
- Broccoli: 375°F for 6-8 minutes
- Brussels Sprouts: 375°F for 8-10 minutes
- Cauliflower: 375°F for 12-15 minutes

Proteins:

- Chicken Breast: 370°F for 22-23 minutes
- Salmon Fillets: 400°F for 7-9 minutes
- Whole Chicken: 360°F for 75 minutes
- Pork Chops: 375°F for 12-15 minutes

Other:

- Keto Bread: 320°F for 3 minutes (to reheat)
- Keto Pizza: 320°F for 8 minutes

Snacks:

- Keto Mozzarella Sticks: 400°F for 6-8 minutes
- Keto Chicken Tenders: 400°F for 14-16 minutes

Remember to always preheat your air fryer for the best results, and shake the basket halfway through cooking for even crispiness. For specific recipes, always check the internal temperature of your food with a meat thermometer to ensure it's cooked through. Adjustments may be needed based on the air fryer model and the size and thickness of your food.

Chapter 19:

Appendix 3. The Dirty Dozen and Clean Fifteen

Whether you're flipping through this cookbook as a keto newbie or a seasoned low-carb chef, knowing which fruits and veggies to pick can make all the difference in your diet. In this appendix, we'll dive into the "Dirty Dozen" and "Clean Fifteen"—your go-to guides for which produce to buy organic and which you can grab from the regular aisle. Let's keep our meals both keto-friendly and clean!

The Dirty Dozen list is published annually by the Environmental Working Group (EWG), highlighting fruits and vegetables with the highest pesticide residues.

On the flip side, the Clean Fifteen is your safest bet if you're looking to save some money while reducing exposure to pesticides.

To ensure you're always armed with the most current information, I've included a QR code below. Scan it to access the latest "Dirty Dozen" and "Clean Fifteen" lists. This way, you can always stay updated with fresh data, which I will continuously update for your convenience.

Navigating the grocery store can be tricky, but here are a few tips to make it easier:

- Look for Labels: USDA Organic is your friend! These products meet strict standards that limit pesticide use.
- Seasonal Shopping: Buying in-season can often mean fresher produce and lower prices for organic items.
- Local Love: Support local farmers' markets where you can often find organic produce that doesn't break the bank.

Happy and healthy eating!

Your feedback is very important to me!
Please scan the QR code below to leave a review.

Printed in Great Britain
by Amazon